THE TESTAMENT
OF
BEAUTY

OXFORD UNIVERSITY PRESS
LONDON : HUMPHREY MILFORD
PUBLISHER TO THE UNIVERSITY

FIRST PRINTED OCTOBER 1929

FOURTEENTH IMPRESSION APRIL 1941

THE TESTAMENT

OF

BEAUTY

A POEM

IN FOUR BOOKS

BY

ROBERT BRIDGES

POET LAUREATE

OXFORD

AT THE CLARENDON PRESS

To The King
G V

ME VERO PRIMVM DVLCES ANTE OMNIA MVSAE
QVARVM SACRA FERO INGENTI PERCVSSVS AMORE
ACCIPIANT.

CONTENTS

THE TESTAMENT

OF BEAUTY

BOOK I

Introduction

MORTAL Prudence, handmaid of divine Providence,
hath inscrutable reckoning with Fate and Fortune:
We sail a changeful sea through halcyon days and storm,
and when the ship laboureth, our stedfast purpose
trembles like as the compass in a binnacle.
Our stability is but balance, and conduct lies
in masterful administration of the unforeseen.

'Twas late in my long journey, when I had clomb to where
the path was narrowing and the company few,
a glow of childlike wonder enthral'd me, as if my sense   10

had come to a new birth purified, my mind enrapt
re-awakening to a fresh initiation of life;
with like surprise of joy as any man may know
who rambling wide hath turn'd, resting on some hill-top
to view the plain he has left, and see'th it now out-spredd
mapp'd at his feet, a landscape so by beauty estranged
he scarce wil ken familiar haunts, nor his own home,
maybe, where far it lieth, small as a faded thought.

   Or as I well remember one highday in June
bright on the seaward South-downs, where I had come afar   20
on a wild garden planted years agone, and fenced
thickly within live-beechen walls: the season it was
of prodigal gay blossom, and man's skill had made
a fair-order'd husbandry of thatt nativ pleasaunce:
But had ther been no more than earth's wild loveliness,
the blue sky and soft air and the unmown flowersprent lawns,
I would hav lain me down and long'd, as then I did,
to lie there ever indolently undisturb'd, and watch
the common flowers that starr'd the fine grass of the wold,
waving in gay display their gold-heads to the sun,   30
each telling of its own inconscient happiness,
each type a faultless essence of God's will, such gems
as magic master-minds in painting or music
threw aside once for man's regard or disregard;

things supreme in themselves, eternal, unnumber'd
in the unexplored necessities of Life and Love.

    To such a mood I had come, by what charm I know not,
where on thatt upland path I was pacing alone;
and yet was nothing new to me, only all was vivid
and significant that had been dormant or dead: 40
as if in a museum the fossils on their shelves
should come to life suddenly, or a winter rose-bed
burst into crowded holiday of scent and bloom.
I felt the domination of Nature's secret urge,
and happy escape therein; as when in boyhood once
from the rattling workshops of a great factory
conducted into the engine-room I stood in face
of the quiet driving power, that fast in nether cave
seated, set all the floors a-quiver, a thousand looms
throbbing and jennies dancing; and I felt at heart   50
a kinship with it and sympathy, as children wil
with amicable monsters: for in truth the mind
is indissociable from what it contemplates,
as thirst and generous wine are to a man that drinketh
nor kenneth whether his pleasur is more in his desire
or in the savor of the rich grape that allays it.

    Man's Reason is in such deep insolvency to sense,

that tho' she guide his highest flight heav'nward, and teach him
dignity morals manners and human comfort,
she can delicatly and dangerously bedizen   60
the rioting joys that fringe the sad pathways of Hell.
Nor without alliance of the animal senses
hath she any miracle: Lov'st thou in the blithe hour
of April dawns—nay marvelest thou not—to hear
the ravishing music that the small birdës make
in garden or woodland, rapturously heralding
the break of day; when the first lark on high hath warn'd
the vigilant robin already of the sun's approach,
and he on slender pipe calleth the nesting tribes
to awake and fill and thrill their myriad-warbling throats   70
praising life's God, untill the blisful revel grow
in wild profusion unfeign'd to such a hymn as man
hath never in temple or grove pour'd to the Lord of heav'n?
    Hast thou then thought that all this ravishing music,
that stirreth so thy heart, making thee dream of things
illimitable unsearchable and of heavenly import,
is but a light disturbance of the atoms of air,
whose jostling ripples, gather'd within the ear, are tuned
to resonant scale, and thence by the enthron'd mind received
on the spiral stairway of her audience chamber   80
as heralds of high spiritual significance?

and that without thine ear, sound would hav no report.
Nature hav no music; nor would ther be for thee
any better melody in the April woods at dawn
than what an old stone-deaf labourer, lying awake
o' night in his comfortless attic, might perchance
be aware of, when the rats run amok in his thatch?

Now since the thoughtless birds not only act and enjoy
this music, but to their offspring teach it with care,
handing on those small folk-songs from father to son   90
in such faithful tradition that they are familiar
unchanging to the changeful generations of men—
and year by year, listening to himself the nightingale
as amorous of his art as of his brooding mate
practiseth every phrase of his espousal lay,
and still provoketh envy of the lesser songsters
with the same notes that woke poetic eloquence
alike in Sophocles and the sick heart of Keats—
see then how deeply seated is the urgence whereto
Bach and Mozart obey'd, or those other minstrels   100
who pioneer'd for us on the marches of heav'n
and paid no heed to wars that swept the world around,
nor in their homes wer more troubled by cannon-roar
than late the small birds wer, that nested and carol'd
upon the devastated battlefields of France.

Birds are of all animals the nearest to men
for that they take delight in both music and dance,
and gracefully schooling leisure to enliven life
wer the earlier artists: moreover in their airy flight
(which in its swiftness symboleth man's soaring thought)   110
they hav no rival but man, and easily surpass
in their free voyaging his most desperate daring,
altho' he hath fed and sped his ocean-ships with fire;
and now, disturbing me as I write, I hear on high
his roaring airplanes, and idly raising my head
see them there; like a migratory flock of birds
that rustle southward from the cold fall of the year
in order'd phalanx—so the thin-rankt squadrons ply,
til sound and sight failing me they are lost in the clouds.

Man's happiness, his flaunting honey'd flower of soul,   120
is his loving response to the wealth of Nature.
Beauty is the prime motiv of all his excellence,
his aim and peaceful purpose; whereby he himself
becoming a creator hath often a thought to ask
why Nature, being so inexhaustible of beauty,
should not be all-beauteous; why, from infinit resource,
produce more ugliness than human artistry
with any spiritual intention can allow?

(6)

Wisdom wil repudiate thee, if thou think to enquire
WHY things are as they are or whence they came: thy task   130
is first to learn WHAT IS, and in pursuant knowledge
pure intellect wil find pure pleasur and the only ground
for a philosophy conformable to truth.
And wouldst thou play Creator and Ordinator of things,
be Nature then thy Chaos and be thou her God!
Whereafter, if in spirit dishearten'd and distress'd
to find evil with good, ugly with beautiful
proffer'd by Nature indifferently without shame,
thou wilt proceed to judge, but in conning thy brief
suspect the prejudice of human self-regard   140
distinguishing moralities where never is none—
thou art come round wrongfully again to question Nature,
who by her own faculty in thee judgeth herself:
    to impugn thy verdict is to unseat thatt judge.
    And science vindicateth the appeal to Reason
which is no less Nature's prescriptiv oracle
for being in all her plan so small and tickle a thing:
    How small a thing! if things immeasurable allow
a greater and less (and thought wil reckon some thoughts great,
prolific, everlasting; other some again   150
small and contemptible) say then, How small a part
of Universal Mind can conscient Reason claim!

'Tis to the unconscious mind as the habitable crust
is to the mass of the earth; this crust whereon we dwell
whereon our loves and shames are begotten and buried,
our first slime and ancestral dust: 'Tis, to compare,
thinner than o'er a luscious peach the velvet skin
that we rip off to engorge the rich succulent pulp:
Wer but our planet's sphere so peel'd, flay'd of the rind
that wraps its lava and rock, the solar satellite   160
would keep its motions in God's orrery undisturb'd.
  Yea: and how delicat! Life's mighty mystery
sprang from eternal seeds in the elemental fire,
self-animat in forms that fire annihilates:
all its selfpropagating organisms exist
only within a few degrees of the long scale
rangeing from measured zero to unimagin'd heat,
a little oasis of Life in Nature's desert;
and ev'n therein are our soft bodies vext and harm'd
by their own small distemperature, nor coud they endure   170
wer't not that by a secret miracle of chemistry
they hold internal poise upon a razòr-edge
that may not ev'n be blunted, lest we sicken and die.

  This Intellect, whereby above the other species

I

Mankind assumeth genus in a rank apart,
is nascent also in brutes, and of their bloodkinship
as fair a warranty as our common passions are,
our common bones and muscles, skin and nerves of sense.
But because human sorrow springeth of man's thought,
some men hav fal'n unhappily to envy the brutes   180
who for mere lack of reason, love life and enjoy
existence without care: and in some sort doubtless
happier are they than many a miserable man,
whether in disease or misfortune outclass'd from life
or thru' the disillusion of Lust wreck'd in remorse:
Corruption of best is ever the worst corruption.

'Tis true ther is no balance to weigh these goods and ills
nor any measur of them, like as of colour and heat
in their degrees; they are incommensurable in kind.
'Tis with mere pleasur and pain as if they, being so light,   190
coud not this way or thatt deflect Life's monarch-beam;
for howso deliberatly a man may wish for death
still wil he instinctivly fight to the last for life.
Yet with the burden of thought pains are of great moment,
and sickening thought itself engendereth corporal pain:
But likewise also of pleasure—here too Reason again,

whether in prospect or memory, is the greater part;
our hope is ever livelier than despair, our joy
livelier and more abiding than our sorrows are,
which leak away untill no taint remain; their seeds   200
shriveling too thin to lodge in Memory's hustled sieve.
Wherefore I assert:—if Reason's only function wer
to heighten our pleasure, thatt wer vindication enough;
For what wer pleasur if never contemplation gave
a spiritual significance to objects of sense,
nor in thought's atmosphere poetic vision arose?

  Brutes hav their keener senses far outrangeing ours
nor without here and there some adumbration of soul:
But the sensuous intuition in them is steril,
'tis the bare cloth whereon our rich banquet is spredd;   210
and so the sorrowful sufferer who envied their state,
wer he but granted his blind wish to liv as they
—whether 'twer lark or lion, or some high-antler'd stag
in startled pose of his fantastic majesty
gazing adown the glade—he would draw blank, nor taste
the human satisfaction of his release from care:
as well be a sloven toad in his dark hole: Unlike
those damn'd souls by the Harpies tantalized in Hell
whose tortur it was to see their ostentatious feast
snatch'd from their reach—but he sitting with the dainties   220

out-spredd before him would see them, nor ever feel
any desire nor memory of their old relish.

    This quarrel and dissatisfaction of man with Nature
springeth of a vision which beareth assurance
of the diviner principle implicit in Life :
And mystic Vision may so wholly absorb a man
that he wil loathe ev'n pleasure, mortifying the flesh
by disciplin of discomfort so to strengthen his faith.
Thus tho' 'twas otherwise than on Plato's ladder
that Francis climb'd—rather his gentle soul had learn'd   230
from taste of vanity and by malease of the flesh—
he abjured as worthless ev'n what good men wil call good,
and standing forth, as chivalrous knight and champion
of holiness, in his devotion of heart to God,
all earthly sun-joys seem'd so transitory and vain
that soon the unseen took shape to common eyes; the folk
cumber'd him with servility, and his memory
is beatified in the admiration of all mankind.
    Now his following in life and his fame thereafter
confute the lower school of Ethick, which would teach   240
that spiritual ideas are but dream-stuff in men:
For Francis admitted no compromise nor gloss
whereby the Church had thought to ease the easy yoke

which he reshoulder'd as his Master had offer'd it,
and espousing Poverty as the outcast widow of Christ
would walk in Umbria as He walk'd in Galilee
founding the kingdom of God among those angry Jews
who made earthly rebellion against Cæsar's empire:
and in imitation and compassion of Jesus
would touch nothing but what had been bless'd at his lips: 250
For the morrow hav no more care than a lily hath—
for his head no more shelter than a beast of the field—
no purse nor scrip for his journey, and but one garment—
and scorning intellect and pursuit of knowledge
liv'd as a bare spirit in its low prison of flesh,
untill thru' tribulation he should win to peace,
quam mundus nobis dare non potest pacem,
in those eternal mansions where Dante found him
among the Just. Yet ev'n Francis coud praise Nature,
tho' from such altitude whatever pictur is drawn   260
must be out of focus of our terrestrial senses.

'Twas thus he made, when he lay sick in Damian,
his hymn in honour of God and praise of his creatures;
All-first and specially of the Sun whom he calleth
his honourable brother and symbol of Very God;
and then the Moon his sister, and all the stars of heav'n
the clouds and winds his kindred; and of the Earth he saith—

Praisèd be thou, my Lord, for my sister, Mother Earth,
who doth sustain and govern us and bringeth forth
all manner of fruit and herb and flowers of myriad hue.   270
In direst pain of body and despond of soul he ask'd
but for this Bencitè to be sung by his bed,
fleeing for sanctuary to the bond of Nature—
"the inconceivable high works unfathomable
    whose aspect giveth the Angels strength, and men
    revere the gentle changes of the day."—

The sky's unresting cloudland, that with varying play
sifteth the sunlight thru' its figured shades, that now
stand in massiv range, cumulated stupendous
mountainous snowbillowy up-piled in dazzling sheen,   280
Now like sailing ships on a calm ocean drifting,
Now scatter'd wispy waifs, that neath the eager blaze
disperse in air; Or now parcelling the icy inane
highspredd in fine diaper of silver and mother-of-pearl
freaking the intense azure; Now scurrying close o'erhead,
wild ink-hued random racers that fling sheeted rain
gustily, and with garish bows laughing o'erarch the land:
Or, if the spirit of storm be abroad, huge molten glooms
mount on the horizon stealthily, and gathering as they climb 289
deep-freighted with live lightning, thunder and drenching flood
rebuff the winds, and with black-purpling terror impend

til they be driven away, when grave Night peacefully
clearing her heav'nly rondure of its turbid veils
layeth bare the playthings of Creation's babyhood;
and the immortal fireballs of her uttermost space
twinkle like friendly rushlights on the countryside.

    Them soon the jealous Day o'errideth to display
Earth's green robe, which the sun fostereth for shelter and shower
The dance of young trees that in a wild birch-spinney
toss to and fro the cluster of their flickering crests,   300
as rye curtseying in array to the breeze of May;
The ancestral trunks that mightily in the forest choirs
rear stedfast colonnade, or imperceptibly
    sway in tall pinewoods to their whispering spires;
The woodland's alternating hues, the vaporous bloom
of the first blushings and tender flushings of spring;
The slumbrous foliage of high midsummer's wealth;
Rich Autumn's golden quittance, to the bankruptcy
of the black shapely skeletons standing in snow:
Or, in gay months of swelling pomp, the luxury   310
of leisur'd gardens teeming with affection'd thought;
the heartfelt secrecy of rustic nooks, and valleys
vocal with angelic rilling of rocky streams,
by rambling country-lanes, with hazel and thorn embower'd
woodbine, bryony and wild roses; the landscape lure

of rural England, that held glory in native art
untill our painters took their new fashion from France.

This spiritual elation and response to Nature
is Man's generic mark. A wolf that all his life
had hunted after nightfall neath the starlit skies   320
should he suddenly attain the first inklings of thought
would feel this Wonder: and by some kindred stir of mind
the ruminants can plead approach—the look of it
is born already of fear and gentleness in the eyes
of the wild antelope, and hence by fable assign'd
to the unseen unicorn reposed in burning lair—
a symbol of majestic sadness and lonely pride:
but the true intellectual wonder is first reveal'd
in children and savages and 'tis there the footing
of all our temples and of all science and art.   330
Thus Rafaël once venturing to show God in Man
gave a child's eyes of wonder to the baby Christ;
and his Mantuan brother coud he hav seen that picture
would more truly hav foreshadow'd the incarnation of God.
'Tis divinest childhood's incomparable bloom,
the loss whereof leaveth the man's face shabby and dull.

SEEKING unceasingly for the First Cause of All,
in question for what special Purpose he was made,
Man, in the unsearchable darkness, knoweth one thing
that as he is, so was he made: and if the Essence   340
and characteristic faculty of humanity
is our conscient Reason and our desire of knowledge,
thatt was Nature's Purpose in the making of man.

But can ther be any Will or Purpose in Nature?
thatt Universe external to our percipient sense,
which when we examin itself we think only to find
a structur of blind atoms to their habits enslaved,
or else, examining our senses, suspect to be
a dream of empty appearance and vain imagery.—
   As a man thru' a window into a darken'd house   350
peering vainly wil see, always and easily,
the glass surface and his own face mirror'd thereon,
tho' looking from another angle, or hooding his eyes
he may discern some real objects within the room—
some say 'tis so with us, and also affirm that they
by study of their reflection hav discover'd in truth
ther is nothing but thatt same reflection inside the house.
   See how they hav made o' the window an impermeable wall
partitioning man off from the rest of nature

with stronger impertinence than Science can allow.   360

Man's mind, Nature's entrusted gem, her own mirror

cannot bë isolated from her other works

by self-abstraction of its unique fecundity

   in the new realm of his transcendent life;—

Not emotion or imagination ethick or art

logic of science nor dialectic discourse,

not ev'n thatt supersensuous sublimation of thought,

the euristic vision of mathematical trance,

hath any other foundation than the common base

of Nature's building:—not even his independence   370

of will, his range of knowledge, and spiritual aim,

can separate him off from the impercipient:

Altho' his mind be such that it might seem as if

true Individuality within the species

were peculiar to man: So foolish is he, and wise,—

despondent and hopeful, patient and complaining,

courageous and cowardly, diffident and vain,

cringing and commanding, industrious and idle,

cruel and tenderhearted, truthful and perfidious,

imaginativ or dull—one man how loveable   380

another how hateful, alike man, brutal or divine.

   Whereamong hath the sceptic honourable place,

thatt old iconoclast who coud destroy the gods

soon as men made them, vain imagery and unworthy,
low symbols of the Eternal that standeth unchanged.
Like some medicinal root in pharmacy, whose juice
is wholesom for purgation,—so is he—and if Truth
be thatt which Omniscience would assert of all things,
we may grant him his motto "Truth is not for man".
But from his sleepy castle he wil be tempted forth   390
if ever a hunting-horn echo in the woods around,
for he loveth the chase, and, like a good sportsman,
his hounds and his weapons as he loveth the prey.

So musing all my days with unceasing wonder
and encountering many phases of many minds,
thru' kindly environment of my disposition
I grew, as all things grow, in the pattern of Self;
til stumbling early upon the mystic words, whereby
—in the Semitic matrix of my father's creed—
Jahveh reveal'd his secret Being to the Jews,   400
and conning those large letters I AM THAT I AM
I wonder'd finding only my own thought of myself,
and reading there that man was made in God's image
knew not yet that God was made in the image of man;
nor the profounder truth that both these truths are one,
no quibbling scoff—for surely as mind in man groweth

so with his manhood groweth his idea of God,
wider ever and worthier, untill it may contain
and reconcile in reason all wisdom passion and love,   409
and bring at last (may God so grant) Christ's Peace on Earth.

Nor coud it ever dwell in my possible thought
that whatsoever grew and groweth can be unlike
in cause and substance to the thing it groweth on:
Thus I saw Conscience as a natural flower-bud
on its vigorous plant specialized to a function
marvelously, a blossom first unique in design
of beauty, in colour and form, thickening therefrom to a fruit
productiv to infinit regeneration; and yet
this bud—as any primer of botany can teach—
is but a differentiation of the infertile leaf,   420
which held all this miracle in intrinsic potence.

Thus science would teach, and Heraclitus, I say,
was not the least among the sages of Hellas,
Nor those fire-worshippers foolish who, seeing the Sun
to be the efficient cause of all life upon earth,
welcomed his full effulgence for their symbol of God.
And since we observe in all existence four stages—
Atomic, Organic, Sensuous, and Selfconscient—
and must conceive these in gradation, it was no flaw
in Leibnitz to endow his monad-atoms with Mind: 430

tho' in our schools of thought "unconscious mind" is call'd
a contradiction in terms; as if the embranglements
of logic wer the prime condition of all Being,
the essence of things; and man in the toilsom journey
from conscience of nothing to conscient ignorance
mistook his tottery crutch for the main organ of life.

'Tis laughable that man should fondle such surprise
at animal behaviour, seeing some beetle or fly
—whose very existence is so negligible and brief—
act more intelligently than he might himself   440
had he been there to advise with all his pros and cons,
his cause, effect and means: Such conduct he wil style
"Marvels of Instinct", but what sort of wisdom is this
that mistaketh the exception for the general rule
and the rule for the exception? Since the animal world
immeasurably outnumbereth the species of man,
and wholly is ruled by Instinct: 'Tis the Reason of man
that is the exception and marvel; nay, 'tis plain to see
how, as our Life is animal so also our conduct
is mainly instinctiv, while pure Reason left to herself   450
relieth on axioms and essential premises
which she can neither question nor resolve, things far
beyond her, holding her anchor in eternal Mind,

characteristic universals, the firm rock
whereon her lofty watch-towers are planted, and all
   her star-gazing observatories built.

  Wise thinkers do homage to good fellow-thinkers,
nor disregard the general commonsense of man
—that untouch'd photograph of external Nature
self-pictur'd for us nakedly on her own mirror:—   460
and tho' common opinion may be assent in error
ther is little or none accord in philosophic thought:
this picklock Reason is still a-fumbling at the wards,
bragging to unlock the door of stern Reality.
Ask what is reasonable! See how time and clime
conform mind more than body in their environment;
what then and there was Reason, is here and now absurd;
what I now chance to approve, may be or become to others
strange and unpalatable as now appear to me
the weighty sentences of the angelic Doctor: 470
For I rank it among the unimaginables
how Saint Thomas, with all his honesty and keen thought,
toiling to found an irrefragable system
of metaphysic, ethic and theologic truth
should with open eyes hav accepted for main premiss
the myth of a divine fiasco, on which to assure

the wisdom of God; leading to a foregon conclusion
of illachrymable logic, a monstrous scheme
horrendum informe ingens cui Lumen ademptum.

    Some would say that the Saint himself held not the faith   480
which universal credit compell'd him to assume
if he would lead and teach the Church: But so to think
(as tho' 'twas but the best gambit to open his game)
wer to his acumen and his honesty alike unjust.
I am happier in surmising that his vision at Mass
—in Naples it was when he fell suddenly in trance—
was some disenthralment of his humanity;
for thereafter, whether 'twer Aristotle or Christ
that had appear'd to him then, he nevermore wrote word
neither dictated but laid by inkhorn and pen;   490
and was as a man out of hearing on thatt day
when Reynaldus, with all the importunity of zeal
and intimacy of friendship, would hav recall'd him
to his incompleted SUMMA; and·sighing he reply'd

   I wil tell thee a secret, my son, constraining thee
lest thou dare impart it to any man while I liv.
My writing is at end. I hav seen such things reveal'd
that what I hav written and taught seemeth to me of small worth.
And hence I hope in my God, that, as of doctrin
   ther wil be speedily also an end of Life!

I

THER is no tradition among the lemmings of Norway
how their progenitors, when their offspring increased,
bravely forsook their crowded nestes in the snow,
swarming upon the plains to ravage field and farm,
and in unswerving course ate their way to the coast,
where plunging down the rocks they swam in the salt sea
to drowning death; nor hav they in acting thus today
any plan for their journey or prospect in the event.

   But clerks and chroniclers wer many in Christendom,
when France and Germany pour'd out the rabblement   510
of the second Crusade, and its record is writ;
its leaders' titles, kings and knights of fair renown,
their resolve and design: and yet for all their vows,
their consecrating crosses and embroider'd flags,
the eloquent preaching of Saint Bernard, and the wiles
of thatt young amorous amazon, Queen Eleanòr,
they wer impell'd as madly, journey'd as blindly
and perish'd as miserably as the thoughtless voles,
by disease starvation and massacre, or enslaved
by wrath of the folk whose homes they had wreckt and ravaged;
til of the unnumber'd rout a poor remnant fled back,   521
the shame of humanity for their folly and crimes.

Reason, shamefast at heart and vain above measure,
would look to find the firstfruits of intelligence
showing some provident correction of man's estate
to'ard social order, a wise discriminat purpose
in clear contrast against the blind habits of brutes:
And when our honest hope turneth away repell'd
by the terror and superstition of savagery
—wherein nascent Reason seemeth to hav hoodwink'd Mind,—
if we read but of Europe since the birth of Christ,   531
'tis still incompetent disorder, all a lecture
of irredeemable shame; the wrongs and sufferings
alike of kings and clowns are a pitiful tale.

Follow the path of those fair warriors, the tall Goths,
from the day when they led their blue-eyed families
off Vistula's cold pasture-lands, their murky home
by the amber-strewen foreshore of the Baltic sea,
and in the incontaminat vigor of manliness
feeling their rumour'd way to an unknown promised land,   540
tore at the ravel'd fringes of the purple power,
and trampling its wide skirts, defeating its armies,
slaying its Emperor, and burning his cities,
sack'd Athens and Rome; untill supplanting Cæsar
they ruled the world where Romans reign'd before:—

Yet from those three long centuries of rapin and blood,
inhumanity of heart and wanton cruelty of hand,
ther is little left, save the broken relic of one
good bishop, and the record of one noble king,
—who both had suck'd their virtue from the wither'd dugs
of learning, where she lay sickening within the walls   551
of rich Byzance:—Those Goths wer strong but to destroy;
they neither wrote nor wrought, thought not nor created;
but since the field was rank with tares and mildew'd wheat,
their scything won some praise: Else hav they left no trace,
save for their share in thatt rich mingled character
of Hebrew, Roman, Vandal, Mussulman and Kelt,
that spoke the pride of Spain, to stand for ever alive
in one grandesque effigy of ennobled folly,
among fair Beauty's fairest offspring unreproved.   560

    Yet for this intellectual laughter—deem it not
true Wisdom's panoply. The wise wil live by Faith,
faith in the order of Nature and that her order is good.
'Twer scepticism in them to cherish make-believe,
creeds and precise focusings of the unsearchable:
at such things they may smile; yet for man's ignorance
and frailty the only saving consolation is faith,
the which theologians tell us is the gift of God,
as other good things are, and laughter is one of them;

and sharing of man's Essence 'twil be at height in him 570
when 'tis the laughter of Reason—enjoyable; and 'tis fit
that he should show Nature this courtesy, and kindly
make light of all the troubles that compel no tears:
—Cervantes in misfortune when a galley-slave
wept not—but where sorrow is sacred humour is dumb,
and in full calamity it is madness: wherefore
Hamlet himself would never hav been aught to us, or we
to Hamlet, wer't not for the artful balance whereby
Shakespeare so gingerly put his sanity in doubt
  without the while confounding his Reason. 580

And tho' desire of perfection is Nature's promise
we should not in the field of Reason look to find
less vary and veer than elsewhere in the flux of Life:
We may rather rejoice in the great abundance,
the indigenous fruitage of our gay Paradise,
that Persia, China and Babylon put forth their bloom,
that India and Egypt wer seedplots of wisdom.
The best part of our lives we are wanderers in Romance:
Our fathers travel'd Eastward to revel in wonders
where pyramid pagoda and picturesque attire 590
glow in the fading sunset of antiquity;
and now wil the Orientals make hither in return

outlandish pilgrimage : their wiseacres hav seen
the electric light i' the West, and come to worship;
tasting romance in our unsightly novelties
and scientific tricks; for all things in their day
may hav opinion of glory : Glory is opinion,
the vain doxology wherewith man would praise God.

Time eateth away at many an old delusion,
yet with civilization delusions make head;   600
the thicket of the people wil take furtiv fire
from irresponsible catchwords of live ideas,
    sudden as a gorse-bush from the smouldering end
of any loiterer's match-splint, which, unless trodden out
afore it spredd, or quell'd with wieldy threshing-rods
wil burn ten years of planting with all last year's ricks
and blacken a countryside. 'Tis like enough that men
ignorant of fire and poison should be precondemn'd
to sudden deaths and burnings, but 'tis mightily
to the reproach of Reason that she cannot save   610
nor guide the herd; that minds who else wer fit to rule
must win to power by flattery and pretence, and so
by spiritual dishonesty in their flurried reign
confirm the disrepute of all authority—
but only in sackcloth can the Muse speak of such things.

(27)

WISDOM HATH HEWED HER HOUSE: She that dwelleth alway
with God in the Evermore, afore any world was,
fashion'd the nascent Earth that the energy of its life
might come to evolution in the becoming of Man,
who, as her subject, should subjéct all to her rule   620
and bring God's latest work to be a realm of delight.
So she herself, the essential Beauty of Holiness,
pass'd her creativ joy into the creature's heart,
to take back from his hand her Adoration robes
and royal crown of his Imagination and Love.

And when she had made of men lovers and worshippers,
these vied to enshrine her godhead in enduring fanes
and architectur of stone, that high her pensiv towers
might hallow their throng'd cities and, transfeaturing
Nature's wilding landscape to the impress of her Mind,   630
comfort man's mortality with immortal grace.

Yet not to those colossal temples where old Nile
guideth a ribbon oasis thru' the Libyan sands,
depositing a kingdom from his fabled fount
—like thatt twin-sister stream of slothful thought, whose flood
fertilized the rude mind of Egypt—not to these,
nor those Cyclopean tombs, which hieroglyphic kings

whose Goddess was ATHENA, met, and in her right
knew themselves lords of Hellas and the Achean land
whereto they had come fighting, for their children to win
heritage of Earth's empire. 'Twas their youthful tongue
that Wisdom sought when her Egyptian kingdom fail'd,
and choosing to be call'd Athena daughter of Zeus
motion'd the marble to her living grace, and took
her dwelling in the high-templed Acropolis
    of the fair city that still hath her name.

  As some perfected flower, Iris or Lily, is born   670
patterning heav'nly beauty, a pictur'd idea
that hath no other expression for us, nor coud hav:
for thatt which Lily or Iris tell cannot be told
by poetry or by music in their secret tongues,
nor is discerptible in logic, but is itself
an absolute piece of Being, and we know not,
nay, nor search not by what creativ miracle
the soul's language is writ in perishable forms—
yet are we aware of such existences crowding,
mysterious beauties unexpanded, unreveal'd,   680
phantasies intangible investing us closely,
hid only from our eyes by skies that wil not clear;
activ presences, striving to force an entrance,

like bodiless exiled souls in dumb urgence pleading
to be brought to birth in our conscient existence,
as if our troubled lot wer the life they long'd for;
even as poor mortals thirst for immortality:—
And every divination of Natur or reach of Art
is nearer attainment to the divine plenitude
of understanding, and in moments of Vision   690
    their unseen company is the breath of Life:—

    By such happy influence of their chosen goddess
the mind of Hellas blossom'd with a wondrous flow'r,
flaming in summer season, and in its autumn fall
ripening an everlasting fruit, that in dying
scatter'd its pregnant seeds into all the winds of heav'n:
nor ever again hath like bloom appear'd among men.

    Knowledge accumulateth slowly and not in vain;
with new attainment new orders of beauty arise,
in thought and art new values; but man's faculties   700
were gifted once for all and stand, 'twould seem, at stay:
Ther is now no higher intellect to brighten the world
than little Hellas own'd; nay scarcely here and there
liveth a man among us to rival their seers.
    So might we fear that such implicit unity,
so friendly a passionat love for nature beauty and truth,

such dignity of the body tender of pride and shame,
such lively accord of Sense, Instinct, Reason and Spirit
as gazeth down on us with alien sovranty
from all their statuesque literature and art,   710
wer a grace (so might we fear) like the grace of childhood
lost in growth, a glory of the past, not to return.
ꞌ Such ꞌtwer vain to deplore; since true beauty of manhood
outfeatureth childish charm, and whether in men or things
Best is mature; thoꞌ Beauty is neither growth nor strength;
for ugliness also groweth proudly and is strong.
Well might we ask what Beauty ever coud liv or thrive
in our crowded democracy under governance
of such politic fancy as a farmer would show
who cultivated weeds in hope of good harvest: 720
and yet hath modern cultur enrichꞌd a wasting soil;
Science comforting manꞌs animal poverty
and leisuring his toil, hath humanized manners
and social temper, and now above her globe-spredd net
of speeded intercourse hath outrun all magic,
and disclosing the secrecy of the reticent air
hath woven a seamless web of invisible strands
spiriting the dumb inane with the quick matter of life:
Now music's prison'd raptur and the drown'd voice of truth
mantled in light's velocity, over land and sea   730

are omnipresent, speaking aloud to every ear,
into every heart and home their unhinder'd message,
the body and soul of Universal Brotherhood;
whereby war faln from savagery to fratricide,
from a trumpeting vainglory to a crying shame,
stalketh now with blasting curse branded on its brow.

And if the Greek Muses wer a graceful company
yet hav we two, that in maturity transcend
the promise of their baby-prattle in Time's cradle,
Musick and Mathematick: coud their wet-nurses   740
but see these foster-children upgrown in full stature,
Pythagoras would marvel and Athena rejoice.

And ev'n to Apollo's choir was a rich voice lacking
in the great symphonies of the poetic throng
who beneath Homer's crown enroll'd immortal names;
for without later names the full compass of song
had been unknown to man—nay and some English names,
whose younger voices in the imagination of love
swell'd to spiritual ecstasy, and emotion'd life
with mystic inspiration of new lyric rapture: 750
and 'twas the first alluring gleam of thatt vision
that stole by virtue of novelty the world away
from the philosophic concinnity of Greek art,
to abjure the severe ordering of its antique folds.

In love of fleshly prowess Hellas overesteem'd
the nobility of passion and of animal strength,
and the acclamation of their Olympic games outfaced
spiritual combat;—as their forefathers wer they,
those old seapirates, who with roving robbery
built up their island lordships on the ruin of Crete,   760
when the unforbearing rivalry of their free cities
wreck'd their confederacy within the sevenscore years
'twixt Marathon and Issus; untill from the pride
of routing Xerxes and his fabulous host, they fell
to make thatt most memorable of all invasions
less memorable in the glory of Alexander,
under whose alien kingship they conspired to outreach
their own ambition, winning dominions too wide
for domination; and wer, with their virtue, dispersed
and molten into the great stiffening alloy of Rome.   770

So it was when Jesus came in his gentleness
with his divine compassion and great Gospel of Peace,
men hail'd him WORD OF GOD, and in the title of Christ
crown'd him with love beyond all earth-names of renown.
For He, wandering unarm'd save by the Spirit's flame,
in few years with few friends founded a world-empire
wider than Alexander's and more enduring;

since from his death it took its everlasting life.
HIS kingdom is God's kingdom, and his holy temple
not in Athens or Rome but in the heart of man.   780
They who understand not cannot forget, and they
who keep not his commandment call him Master and Lord.
He preach'd once to the herd, but now calleth the wise,
and shall in his second Advent, that tarried long,
be glorified by the Greeks that come to the feast:
But the great Light shineth in great darkness, the seed
that fell by the wayside hath been trodden under foot,
thatt which fell on the Rock is nigh wither'd away;
While loud and louder thro' the dazed head of the SPHINX
    the old lion's voice roareth o'er all the lands.   790

THE TESTAMENT

OF BEAUTY

BOOK II

Selfhood

T̶HE VISION OF THE SEER who saw the Spirit of Man.
A chariot he beheld speeding twixt earth and heaven
drawn by wing'd horses, and the charioteer thereon
upright with eyes upon the goal and mind alert
controlling his strong steeds, that spurn'd the drifted cloud
as now they sank now mounted in their heav'nward flight.

Thus Plato recordeth—how Socrates told it
to Phædrus on a summer morning, as they sat
beneath a lofty plane-tree by the grassy banks
of the Ilissus, talking of the passions of men.   10

The Vision of the Seer is Truth's Apocalypse,
yet needeth for our aid a true interpreter.
The names of the two horses are SELFHOOD and BREED,
the charioteer is REASON, and the whip in his hand
is not to urge-on the steeds nor to incite their blood;
their mettle is everlasting and they need no goad:
He wieldeth it to make them ware of his presence
and hold them obedient to the rein of his Will.
But this picture drafted in Mind's creativ cave,
and thence on the eye projected, thin is as the film   20
of colour and shade on a canvas, ther is nought beneath:
it telleth not who bred those wild horses, or broke
their strong necks to the yoke, nor who builded the car,
and harness'd them therto for its high heav'nly flight;
nor how REASON ever mounted it in full career
and took the reins, nor of what stuff intangible
they are woven, those reins pictured so taut in his grasp;
nay, for not he himself kenneth well of these things:
Yet truly is he portray'd fearless and glad of heart,
his lash circling o'erhead, as smiling on his steeds   30
he speaketh to them lovingly in his praise or blame.

Now these two horses, without which the wheels of Life
would never hav had motion, and with them can hav no rest,

are the animal instincts in the birthright of man;
nor are they, as Plato fancied, one evil and one good:
both are good, but of their wildness they are restiv both
and wilful, nor wil yield mastery, unless they feel
the hand of expert manage and good horsemanship.
Selfhood is the elder and stronger; but Breed, once her foal,
is livelier and of limb finer and more mettlesome,   40
her rival now, and both wil pull together as one.
    'Tis first to tell of Selfhood, since the first one thing,
if ever a first thing wer, was of the Essence of Self.

    Consider a plant—its life—how a seed faln to ground
sucketh in moisture for its germinating cells,
and as it sucketh swelleth, til it burst its case
and thrusting its roots downward and spreading them wide
taketh tenure of the soil, and from ev'ry raindrop
on its dribbling passage to replenish the springs
plundereth the freighted salt, while it pricketh upright   50
with its flagstaff o'erhead for a place in the sun,
anon to disengage buds that in tender leaves
unfolding may inhale provender of the ambient air:
and, tentacles or tendrils, they search not blindly
but each one headeth straightly for its readiest prey;

and haply, if the seed be faln in a place of darkness
roof'd in by men—if ther should be any ray or gleam
how faint soe'er, 'twil crane and reach its pallid stalk
pushing at the crevice ev'n to disrupt the stones.

'Tis of such absolute selfhood that it knoweth not   60
parent nor offspring, and will abuse advantage
of primogeniture, with long luxuriant boughs
crowding in vain-glory to overshadow and quell
its younger brethren; while, as for its own children
that, cradled on its branches, fell from its fruitage,
'twil choke them when they strive to draw life at its feet.

Look now upon a child of man when born to light,
how otherwise than a plant sucketh he and clutcheth?
how with his first life-breath he clarioneth for food!
craving as the blind fledgelings in a thrush's nest   70
that perk their naked necks, stiff as a chimney-stack,
food-funnels, like as hoppers in a corn-mill gaping
for what supply the feeder may shovel in their throats.
How differeth the new-born child from plant or fledgeling?

Among low organisms some are call'd animal
for being unrooted, else inseparable from plants;
yet each in his small motion is as a lion on prowl,
or as a python gliding to seize and devour
some weaker Self, whereby to fortify his own.

And if Selfhood thus rule thru'out organic life   80
'tis no far thought that all the dumb activities
in atom or molecule are like phenomena
of individuat Selfhood in its first degrees.

   This Autarchy of Selfhood, which we blame not at all
in plants and scarcely in brutes, is by Reason denounced
heartless, and outlaw'd from the noble temper of man,
the original sin and cause of half his woes and shames;
whence Natur again would seem at variance with herself,
misdoubting the foundation whereon she had built all,
and seeing too late the fault threating to split her house   90
would buttress it with the outwork of an afterthought.
But tho 'tis only Reason can govern this horse,
correction awaited not the human charioteer;
Selfhood had of itself begotten its own restraint—
like as small plague-microbes generate their own toxin
in antidote of their own mischief (so 'tis said):
Even among beasts ot prey the bloody wolves, who found
some selfish betterment from their hunting in packs,
had thereby learn'd submission to a controlling will,
their leader being so far charioteer of their rage;   100
while pastoral animals, or ever a drover came
to pen them for his profit, had in self-defence

herded together; and on the wild prairies are seen
when threaten'd by attack, congregating their young
within their midst for safety, and then serrying their ranks
in a front line compact to face the dreaded foe.

And this parental instinct, tho' it own cousinship
with Breed, was born of Selfhood. A nursing mammal,
since she must feel her suckling a piece of herself,
wil self-preserve and shelter it as herself; and oft   110
'tis hard to wean. So birds, by long brooding inured,
wil watch their chickens heedfully, and fearfully attend
their early excursions, guiding aiding and at need
defending against danger. It is pretty to mark
a partridge, when she hath first led forth her brood to run
among the grass-tussocks or hay-stubbles of June,
if man or beast approach them, how to usurp regard
she counterfeiteth the terror of a wounded bird
draggling a broken wing, and noisily enticeth
or provoketh the foe to follow her in a vain chase;   120
nor wil she desist from the ruse of her courage
to effect her own escape in loud masterful flight,
untill she hav far decoy'd hunter or blundering hoof
from where she has bid her little ones to scatter and hide.

In man this blind motherly attachment is the spring

of his purest affection, and of all compassion,—
the emotion most inimical to war: I deem
its form of unimpeachable sincerity
to be the mould wherein Friendship's full faith is cast.
But richest fruits are tardy in ripening, and man's mind   130
on the last topmost branch, fed from the deepest root,
struggleth slowly to birth thru' long-enforced delay.
See nature's habit now devolving upon man,
and in his Reason her patience as virtue reborn.
First wil be many months of bodily helplessness,
then many years ere the fine budding spirit unclose.
Wherewhile a new spiritual personality
in its miraculous significance, the child
is less the mother's own than a treasur entrusted,
which she can never love too fondly or serve too well;   140
Nay, rather is she possess'd by her own possession,
and in her VITA NUOVA *such things are reveal'd*
that all she hath thought or done seemeth to her of small worth.
The unfathomable mystery of her awaken'd joy
sendeth her daily to heaven on her knees in prayer:
and watching o'er the charm of a soul's wondering dawn
enamoureth so her spirit, that all her happiness
is in her care for him, all hope in his promise;
and his nobility is the dream-goal of her life.

In the sunshine of her devotion, her peace and joy ' 150
are mirror'd in the child's mind, and would leave thereon
no place for sin, coud all be purified to attain;
but in the most the mind is gross and the spirit bleak;
and for a generation needing an outward sign
of this transcendent mystery, 'twas well when Art
fashioning a domestic symbol in worship of Christ
pictured him as an infant in his Mother's arms,
sharing with her his suffering and glory—it was well:
Nor count I any scripture to be better inspired
with eternal wisdom or by insight of man 160
than the four words wherewith the sad penitent hymn
calleth aloud on Mary standing neath the cross:
EIA MATER, it saith, MATER FONS AMORIS.

Leave Selfhood now in her fond sanctuary awhile
with the unseen universe communing and entranced
strangely:—As when a high moon thru' the rifted wrack
gleameth upon the random of the windswept night;
or as a sunbeam softly, on early worshippers
at some rich shrine kneeling, stealeth thru' the eastern apse
and on the clouded incense and the fresco'd walls 170
mantleth the hush of prayer with a vaster silence,
laden as 'twer with the unheard music of the spheres;

—nay, incommunicable and beyond all compare
are the rich influences of those moments of bliss,
mocking imagination or pictured remembrance,
as a divine dream in the vaulted slumber of life.

Leave we Selfhood now secretly under thatt nimbus,
fashioning by nurtur in a new selfhood of spirit
whatever in the redemption of beauty and dignity
ennobleth the society or the person of man—   180
leave thatt nursery awhile, and ask how Nature wrought
where she with-held from life the gift of Motherhood.

The teeming progeny of such egg-breeding insects
as multiply their children a thousandfold a day
must lie close on the zero of parental bondage;
nor can they be debarr'd by ignominy of rank
or unlikeness of kind from vouching in this case:
For among Bees and Ants are social systems found
so complex and well-order'd as to invite offhand
a pleasant fable enough: that once upon a time,   190
or ever a man was born to rob their honeypots,
bees wer fully endow'd with Reason and only lost it
by ordering so their life as to dispense with it;
whereby it pined away and perish'd of disuse,

which, whether it wer or no, if men can judge of Bees,
well might be in their strange manner of life—so like it is
with what our economical bee-minded men
teach as the first intelligential principle
of human government welfare and happiness;—
Nay, some I hav seen wil choose a beehive for their sign   200
and gloss their soul-delusion with a muddled thought,
picturing a skep of straw, the beekeeper's device,
a millowner's workshop, for totem of their tribe;
Not knowing the high goal of our great endeavour
is spiritual attainment, individual worth,
at all cost to be sought and at all cost pursued,
to be won at all cost and at all cost assured;
not such material ease as might be attain'd for all
by cheap production and distribution of common needs,
wer all life level'd down to where the lowest can reach: 210
Thus generating for ever in his crowded treadmills,
man's life wer cheap as bees'; and we may see in them
how he likewise might liv, if each would undertake
the maximum of toil that is found tolerable
upon a day-doled minimum of sustenance;
and stay from procrëation at thatt just number of men,
hard-workers and small-eaters, who coud crowd on earth
under the shadow of this skeleton of happiness.

II

And since life must lose value in diminution of goods,
life-time must also itself be in due proportion abredged;   220
and both diminishings must at some point be stay'd,
lest by slow loss they come dwindling in the end to nought:
then, when to each single life the allotted span is fix'd,
the system wil be at balance, stable and perfected.

   The ground-root folly of this pitous philanthropy
is thinking to distribute indivisibles,
and make equality in things incommensurable:
forged under such delusions, all Utopias
are castles in the air or counsels of despair.
So Plato, on whose infant lips—as it is told—   230
bees settled where he lay slumbering in his cradle,
and honour'd with their augury man's loan of praise—
ev'n Plato, when he in fear and mistrust of Selfhood
denyeth family life to his republicans,
fell, bruized; tho' cautiously depicting Socrates
reluctant to disclose the offensiv absurdum
of his pretentious premiss—when, being forced to admit
that in his free community of women and children
no child would ken its parent, no parent his child,
he sought to twist the bull's horns with a sophistry—   240
arguing that mother's love and home-life being the source

of such inestimable good, 'twer wise that law
should forbid privat property in their benefits:
Nay, so 'twould set his state above all other states,
wer suchlike indispensable privileges
rescued from ownership, and for the general use
distributed equally among the citizens.
For surely (said he) a bastard nursed in a bureau
must love and reverence all women for its mothers;
and likewise every woman, being in like default,   250
would love all babies as her only son. May-be
Plato was pleased to launch his whole Utopia
safely in absolute dreamland; but poor Socrates,
on whom he father'd it, was left *in nubibus*
where Aristophanes in good jest had set him
some twenty years afore: and our sophists, who lack
claim to any shred of great Plato's glorious mantle
of wisdom, hav secured a good lien on his bluff.

But yet to read the strange riddle of the hiving bees,
their altruism and platonesque intelligence,   260
'tis enough to suppose that their small separat selves
are function'd by the same organic socialism
and vital telepathy as the corpuscles are
whereof their little bodies are themselves composed:

that this cell-habit, spredd thru'out to a general sense,
inspireth them in their corporat community.

   Consider the tiny egg-cell whence the man groweth,
how it proliferateth freely, as a queen-bee doth,
and more surely than any animal or plant breedeth;
how each new offspring cell is for some special work   270
differentiated and functioneth spontaneously,
and ev'n wil change its predetermin'd faculty
when accidental environment maketh a call,
leaving its proper sphere to amend what hath gone wrong:
Consider then their task, those unimaginable
infinit co-adaptations of function'd tissue
correlated delicately in a ravel'd web
of unknown sensibilities . . how 'tis a task
incomparable in complexity with whatsoe'er
the bees can boast: nor do the unshapely cells behave   280
with lesser show of will, nor of purpose and skill:
Pass by the rarer achievements, yea, forget all fames,
all works all art all virtue and knowledge—set them by,
and still the solved problems must exhaust our wonder;
Reason can bring no more; and it addeth nothing
that the complete insect should in some part possess
some of the faculties of its constituent cells.
Or if this thing be deem'd in Natur anomalous,

that perfect organisms with sense and motion endow'd
should still behave to each other as link'd constructiv cells,
yet outwardly to our eyes this freedom affordeth   291
machinery wherupon common purpose can work:
To the insect, order and disorder are exposed to sight;
and so we think to see the little emmets confer
and locking their antennæ immediatly transmit
the instinctiv calls which each and all can feel; whereas
the mutual fellowship of distributed cells
hath so confounded thought that explanation is fetch'd
from chemic agency: because in that science
the reaction of unknown forces is described and summ'd   300
in mathematic formulæ pregnant of truth,
and of such universal scope that, being call'd laws,
their mere description passeth for Efficient Cause.

Sometimes when slowly from the deep sleep of fatigue
a man awakeneth, he lyeth for awhile amazed,
aware of self and of his rested body, and yet
knowing not where he is, bewilder'd, unable
to interpret sight or sound, because the slumbering guards
in Memory's Castle hav lagg'd at his summons
for to let down the drawbridge and to uplift the gate: 310

Anon with their deliverance he cometh again
to usual cognisance of the things about him,
life, and all his old familiar concepts of home.

So 'tis with any Manchild born into the world,
so wondereth he awhile at the stuff of his home,
so, tho' slowly and unconsciently, he remembereth.—
The senses ministrant on his apperception
are predisposed to the terrestrial influences,
adapted to the environment where they took shape:
With ease of long habit his lungs inhale the air,   320
his eyes and skin welcome the sun, and his palate
findeth assurance taking to the mother's milk:
His muffling wraps, his frill'd and closely curtain'd cot
and silken apparel of wealth are stranger things to him
than the rough contacts wherefrom they are thought to shield him,
the everlasting companions of his lang syne;
nor later wil he meet with any older acquaintance
than Bees are; for his ancestors ere they wer men
had pillaged the wild combs, and thru' untold ages
hive-honey in cave and palace hath sweeten'd man's food: 330
not all the flooding syrup from the East-Indian cane
foster'd in the Antilles, Ohio and Illinois,
in Java, Demerara or Jamaica can drown
Hybla's renown, nor cheapen the honey of Narbonne:

A jar of Hymettan from a scholar in Athens
regaled our English laurel above all gifts to me,
who hav come to wiser affection in my regard for bees,
learning the secret purpose wherefor Nature plann'd
their industry, and controll'd its fashion to subserve
the beauty and fertility of her vegetant life,   340
to enrich her blooms with colour and fructify her fruits,
—which never a bee can guess, nor that the unwholesomeness
of mixy pollen (a thing that so concerneth bees)
was by the flowers contrived for their own benefit:—

   Nay, whether it be in the gay apple-orchards of May,
when the pink bunches spread their gold hearts to the sun,
nor yet rude winds hav snow'd their petals to the ground;
or when a dizzy bourdon haunteth the sweet cymes
that droop at Lammas-tide the queenly foliage
of a tall linden tree, where yearly by the wall   350
of some long-ruin'd Abbey she remembereth her
of glad thanksgivings and the gay choral Sabbaths,
while in her leafy tower the languorous murmur
floateth off heav'nward in a mellow dome of shade;—
or when, tho' *summer hath o'erbrim'd their clammy cells*
the shorten'd days are shadow'd with dark fears of dearth,
bees ply the more, issuing on sultry noons to throng
in the ivy-blooms—what time October's flaming hues

surcharge the brooding hours, till passionat soul and sense
blend in a rich reverie with the dying year;—   360
when and wherever bees are busy, it is the flowers
dispense their daily task and determin its field;
the prime motiv, may-hap, of all bee-energy,
as of bee-industry they are surely the whole stuff.
Unwitting tho' it is, this great labor of love
in such kindly intimacy with nature's workings
hath a genial beauty, the charm whereof lacketh
to the hireling drudgery of our huge city hives.
So for their happy demeanour and sweet ministry
they wer ever admired of man, and won immortal place   370
in divine story and in poetic fable and rhyme:
Deem'd heav'nly visitants wer they, children of the air
of no earthly engendering, under celestial laws
living a life of wisdom pleasur and diligence,
a model for the polity and society of men.

Alas, we hav seen too near the poor life of the Bee,
how of the swarming workers that cluster'd to found
the pringtide colony and project its waxen walls
not one liveth to sing her *nisi Dominus,*
nor to rest from her labour, nor to enjoy the fruits.   380
Forty days, six unsabbath'd weeks of fever'd toil,

wasteth and wearieth out their little frames—in truth
their eggs wer a mass-product, not design'd to endure,
nor for themselves, but pennywise to serve a turn:—
One by one they succumb on their lonely journeys,
o'erladen above their strength, benighted or astray,
entrapp'd by swooping beaks, or by hard hail laid low
with broken wings, untill a frail remnant at last
wearily welcoming the dim prescience of death
seek their own cemetery, where their shriveling skins   390
may lie together apart nor soil the hive; yet stil
ever and ever as they fail, perish and disappear,
new shifts of younger workers, born of later eggs,
take-up the unresting labour, each in their turn content
   to keep hive clean, eggs plenty, and storeroom full.
Thus passeth summer, and with her draggled pageantry
they too giv o'er, and stay all business in the hive,
and huddling upon the foodstore in their dark den
by numb stagnation husband the low flicker of life,
sustain'd by an unheard promise that their prison again   400
shall feel the sun, and they with the brave buds of March
shall drink the valiance of his steepening rays, they too
be hearten'd to revive, and venturing forth renew
the well-worn round of toil; wherein ther is no one point
of true accomplishment, since the sweet honeycomb

for which man thanketh them, is but their furnishment,
the larder and nursery and provisional shelter
wherein their forlorn hope, their last shift may hold out
thru' the long sleepless night of winter's starving gloom.

    And for their monarch Queen—an egg-casting machine,   410
helpless without attendance as a farmer's drill,
by bedels driven and gear'd and in the furrows steer'd,
well-watch'd the while, and treated with respect and care
so long as she run well, oil'd stoked and kept in trim;
but if deranged she slacken in her depositing,
she is dealt with as men scrap a worn-out seed-barrow,
not worth the mending; new machines cost nought to bees.

    Now when this story is with man's tender sentiment
foolishly travestied, Nature wil seem malign:
But bees—unless the Selfhood of the hive can feel—   420
lack conscience of emotion, or hav no more than when,
call'd by the sun to swarm in a bright morn of May,
their agitated clamour and frolic flight would shew
that some levity hath prick'd their cores: even as with us
who feel the exhilaration of the voluptuous air
that surgeth in our flesh to flood the soul, and ease
our stiff behaviour; and to such happy influences
swarming bees are responsiv and forget to sting:

in which, as in their stranger mockeries of mankind,
they are truly less like us than we are like to them.   430
So all barbaric tyrants, who secure their throne
by murder of rivals, hav their model in the Queen-bee;
and the class-hate that kindleth in disorder'd times,
when prosperity hath set envy and desire at war—
'tis like the workers' annual massacre of the Drones:
And even if some faint rebel mote of pleasure lurk
in these fly-puppetries of human crime, 'tis plain
that bees in their short life can hav so little joy
and so much toil,—I say 'tis plain, that (if the things
be comparable) then with the beehive compared   440
the New-world slave-plantations wer abodes of bliss.

Me-seemeth in my poem these poor hive-bees fare
as with an old black bear that hath climb'd on their tree
in the American Adirondacks or Asian
Himalaya, and clawing their comb, eateth it in,
grubs, bees and honey and all: it is all one to him,
for the brute is omnivorous and hath a sweet tooth.

Conscient Reason, the channel of man's spiritual joy,
hath such dominant function also in bodily feeling
that 'tis the measur of suffering in all animals,   450

in lower forms negligible, and in the lowest
pain can be felt no more than mid the dancing waves
a pleasure-boat feeleth the hand on her tiller
that keepeth-up her head to th' wind and her sails full.
And of spiritual pain the most cometh again
thru' Reason, whether of frailty or of imperfection:—
Savagery hath the throes; and ah! in tender years
the mind of childhood knoweth torments of terror,
fears incommunicable, unconsolable,
vague shapes; tho' oft they be the dread boding of truth,   460
against which man's full Reason at grips may wrestle in vain.
Yet for the gift of his virgin intelligence
a child is ever our nearest pictur of happiness:
'tis a delight to look on him in tireless play
attentivly occupied with a world of wonders,
so rich in toys and playthings that naked Nature
wer enough without the marvelous inventary of man ;
wherewith he toyeth no less, and learning soon the lore
of cypher and·alphabet anon getteth to con
the fair scholarly comment that science hath penn'd   470
glossing the mazy hieroglyph of Nature's book;
and as he ever drinketh of the living waters
his spirit is drawn into the stream and, as a drop
commingled therewith, taketh of birthright therein

as vast an heritage as his young body hath
in the immemorial riches of mortality.

  And now full light of heart he hath willingly pass'd out
thru' the sword-gates of Eden into the world beyond:
He wil be child no more: in his revel of knowledge
all the world is his own: all the hope of mankind   480
is sharpen'd to a spearpoint in his bright confidence,
as he rideth forth to do battle, a Chevalier
in the joyous travail of the everlasting dawn:
Ther is nought to compare then, truly nought to compare:
and wer not Fortune fickle in her lovingkindness,
all wer well with a man—for his life is at flower,
nor hath he any fear: πόθεν θανάτου νῦν
μνημονεύσειεν ἀν ἐν ἀκμῇ τοσαύτῃ?
But since her favor is inscrutable and uncertain,
and of her multiplicity she troubleth not .   490
at the interaction of diverse self-consequences,
ther wil be blastings and blightings of hope and love,
and rude shocks that affray; yet to the enamour'd soul
evil is irrelevant and wil be brush'd aside:
rather 'tis as with Art, wherein special beauty
springeth of obstacles that hav been overcome
and to graces transform'd; so too the lover in life
wil make obstructions serve, and from all resistance

gain strength : his reconcilement with suffering is eased
by fellow-suffering, and in pride of his calling   500
good warriorship welcometh the challenge of death.

Beneath the spaceless dome of the soul's firmament
he liveth in the glow of a celestial fire,
fed by whose timeless beams our small obedient sun
is as a cast-off satellite, that borroweth
from the great Mover of all; and in the light of light
man's little works, strewn on the sands of time, sparkle
like cut jewels in the beatitude of God's countenance.

But heav'nward tho' the chariot be already mounted,
'tis Faith alone can keep the charioteer in heart—   510
Nay, be he but irresolute the steeds wil rebel,
and if he looketh earthward they wil follow his gaze;
and ever as to earth he neareth, and vision cleareth
of all that he feareth, and the enemy appeareth
waving triumphant banners on the strongholds of ill,
his mirroring mind wil tarnish, and mortal despair
possess his soul : then surely Nature hath no night
dark as thatt black darkness that can be felt: no storm
blind as the fury of Man's self-destructiv passions,
no pestilence so poisonous as his hideous sins.   520
Thus men in slavery of sorrow imagin ghastly creeds,
monstrous devilry, abstractions of terror, and wil *look*

to death's benumbing opium as their only cure,
or, seeking proudly to ennoble melancholy
by embracement, wil make a last wisdom of woe:
They lie in Hell like sheep, death gnaweth upon them;
whose prophet sage and preacher is the old Ecclesiast
pseudo-Solomon, who cryeth in the wilderness,
calling all to baptism in the Slough of Despond:
VANITAS VANITATUM, OMNIA VANITAS.   530

——————

THE Spartan General BRASIDAS, the strenuous man,
who earn'd historic favour from his conquer'd foe,
once caught a mouse foraging in his messbasket
among the figs, but when it bit him let it go,
praising its show of fight in words that Plutarch judged
worth treasuring; and since I redd the story at school
unto this hour I hav never thought of Brasidas
and cannot hear his name, but that I straightway see
a table and an arm'd man smiling with hand outstretch'd
above a little mouse that is scampering away.   540
    Why should this thing so hold me? and why do I welcome now
the tiny beast, that hath come running up to me
as if here in my cantos he had spied a crevice,
and counting on my friendship would make it his home?

(60)

'Tis such a pictur as must by mere beauty of fitness
convince natural feeling with added comfort.
The soldier seeth the instinct of Sélfhood in the mouse
to be the same impulse that maketh virtue in him.
For Brasidas held that courage ennobleth man,
and from unworth redeemeth, and that folk who shrink   550
from ventur of battle in self-defence are thereby doom'd
to slavery and extinction: and so this mouse, albeit
its little teeth had done him a petty hurt, deserved
liberty for its courage, and found grace in man.

　I had disliked Brasidas if he had kill'd the mouse :
needless taking of life putteth Reason to shame,
and men so startle at bloodshed that all homicide
may to a purist seem mortal pollution of soul ;
a mystical horror of it may rule in him so strong,
that rather than be slayer he would himself be slain :   560
But fatherhood dispenseth with this vain taboo:
the duty of mightiness is to protect the weak :
and since slackness in duty is unto noble minds
a greater shame and blame than any chance offence
ensuing on right conduct, this hath my assent,—
that where ther is any savagery ther wil be war :
the warrior therefore needeth no apology.

CHILDREN, for all their innocency and gentleness,
in their unreason'd Selfhood think no scorn of war,
but practise mimicry of it in their merry games,   570
like puppies that would learn their fighting tricks betimes;
and a Duke's well-bred cubs win romantic escape
from their palatial mansion, hiding in the woods
where they may scream and weave their raw wigwams, and don
the feathery tinsel and warpaint of the Cherokees.

   My little chorister, who never miss'd a note,—
I mark'd him how when prayers wer ended he would take
his Bible, and in his corner ensconced would sit and read
with unassumed devotion. What was it fetch'd him?
Matthew Mark Luke and John was it? The parables,   580
the poetry and passion of Christ? Nay 'twas the bloody books
of Jewish war, the story of their Judges and Kings;
lured by those braggart annals, while he conn'd the page
the parson's mild discourse pass'd o'er his head unheard.
For Coverdale in his grand English truly built
a temple fair as thatt Ionic fane, wherein
neath his nine-column'd portico of all history
Herodotus sitteth statued; and like the Jew
the naive Greek chronicler discovereth God's purpose
guiding his chosen race to terrestrial glory.   590
Nor hath any other nation any better argument,

whether it be forged or filch'd, invented or stolen;
and their historians all are as children in this,
and eagerly from battlefield to battlefield
jaunt on their prancing pens after their man of war,
who carveth the Earth into new kingdoms, as a cake
is sliced for grabbing school-boys at a teaparty:
and in their exaltation of dread and derringdo,
prowess is magnified and cruelty condoned;
whence smaller nations, as the Portuguese, require   600
to multiply tenfold the tale of combatants,
ere they deem any event worthy of their pictured pride.
Parisian vanity reposeth thus today
on Buonaparte's fame; for Alexander and he
are kings of kings and lords of lords, the conquerors
of conquerors all; dwarfing rude rivals whensoe'er,
Alaric, Tamurlane, Attila and Zingis Khan,
once names of terror and furious bombast, foremost men
humbled, as wer the seventy kings who with their thumbs
and their great toes cut off, finger'd the crumbs beneath   610
Adonibezek's table, untill Jew Simeon came
and did the same by him to my chorister's joy.

And since all earthly EMPIRE hath taken origin
from bloody invasion, man for himself would fashion

his sanction and examplar in the kingdom of heav'n;

Thus hundred-handed giants, swarming from chaos

to exalt the glory of Zeus, barricaded his throne,

uprooting mountains in titanic rebellion.

So hath the Church utter'd like false moneys for Christ

with Godhead's image stamp'd, and pass'd it on the folk   620

who, shadow'd in the murk of vulgar vainglories,

wil prick their ears to hear how "Ther was war in Heav'n,

and Michael and his Angels (like knights of romance)

fought with the Dragon": tho' Almight hath nought to gain,

and by sovran oppression exalteth only his foe

in tragic sympathy, as with Milton's great devil,

against infinit odds confronting undismay'd

inevitable ruin; or old Methusalah

who when the flood rose higher swam from peak to peak

til, with the last wild beasts tamed in their fear, he sat   630

watching the whelm of water on topmost Everest,

as thatt too was submerged; while in his crowded ark

Noah rode safely by: and sailors caught by storm

on the wide Indian Ocean at shift of the monsoon,

hav seen in the dark night a giant swimmer's head

that on the sequent billows trailing silvery hair

at every lightning flash reappeareth in place,

out-riding the tempest, as a weather-bound barque

anchor'd in open roadstead lifteth at the seas.

And POETRY in her task of adorning spirit,   640
trustful also and faithful to the instincts of man,
honoureth ever the steeds above the charioteer.
She once would favour Selfhood, but 'tis now the foal;
and learning sapphic languor in the labour of love,
the Muse hath doff'd her armour for a silken robe:
yet in her swooning luxury she hath never match'd
nor disthroned bearded Homer's great epic of war;
altho' thatt siege of Troy was in the beginning
wrath and concupiscence, and in the end thereof
tragedy so tearful that no mind can approve,   650
nor any gentle heart take comfort in the event.
   But these and all old tales of far-off things, bygones
of long-ago whereof memory still holdeth shape,
Time and the Muse hav purged of their unhappiness;
with their bright broken beauty they pervade the abyss,
peopling the Solitude with gorgeous presences:
as those bare lofty columns, time-whiten'd relics
of Atlanteän adoration, upstanding lone
in Baalbec or Palmyra, proudly affront the waste
and with rich thought atone the melancholy of doom.   660
   Yet since of all, whatever hath once been, evil or good,

tho' we can think not of it and remember it not,

nothing can wholly perish; so ther is no birthright

so noble or stock so clean, but it transmitteth dregs,

contamination at core of old brutality;

inchoate lobes, dumb shapes of ancient terror abide:

tho' fading still in the ocëanic deeps of mind

their eyeless sorrows haunt the unfathom'd density,

dulling the crystal lens of prophetic vision,

crippling the nerve that ministereth to trembling strength,

distorting the features of our nobility: 671

And we, living at prime, what is it now to us

how our forefathers dream'd, suffer'd, struggled, or wrought?

how thru' the obliterated æons of man's ordeal

unnumber'd personalities separatly endured?

Think not to explore, estimate and accumulate

those infinit dark happenings into a single view

that might affect feeling with true judgment of thought:

Imagination, that would set science that task,

is as the astronomer who, with peduncled eye   680

screw'd here or there at some minutest angle-space

of the wide heav'ns, thinketh by piecemeal reckoning

to pictur and comprehend the illimitable worlds

thronging eternity; his highest fantasy

is like an athlete's dream that he hath lept off the globe.

when all his waking power is to jump-up and fall
the height of his own head—all that the best can do.

Wer it not then well to enquire of Reason, ere we admit
her condemnation of War, seeing it so firmly entrench'd
in the immemorial practice and good favour of man,   690
whence hath she fetch'd her high authority, her right
of spiritual judgment? WHENCE THEN COMETH WISDOM?

But I was anger'd with myself to hav said this thing,
seeing that my thought had wander'd; for Reason reply'd
"This question is wrongly ask'd. Who is it that putteth
"this question into my mouth, and biddeth me answer him?—
"I who hav never doubted of my authority,
"who am the consciousness of things judging themselves—
"Hav I not learn'd that Selfhood is fundamental
"and universal in all individual Being;   700
"and that thru' Motherhood it came in animals
"to altruistic feeling, and thence-after in men
"rose to spiritual affection? What then am I
"in my conscience of self but very consciousness
"of spiritual affection upgrown to life in me?
"Truly inscrutable and dark is the Wisdom of God,
"but no man cometh unto WISDOM but by me."

Then was I shamed: but still my thought went harking back
on its old trail, whence Reason learn'd its troublous task
to comprehend aright and wisely harmonise   710
the speechless intuitions of the inconscient mind;
which, tho' a naked babe (as men best pictured Christ)
is yet in some sort nearer to the Omniscient
than man's unperfect Reason, baulk'd as thatt must be
by the self-puzzledom of introspection and doubt.
Thatt dark mind with its potency is the stuff of life,
nature's immutable provision: in some maybe,
stagnant and poor, in some activ and rich, in each
a given unique quantum of personality,
a loan of so-much (as 'tis writ *to one he gave*   720
five talents, to another two and to another one);
a treasure that can be to good fortune assured
by Reason, its determinant and inexplicable
coefficient, that varieth also in power and worth.

For I think not of Reason as men thought of Adam,
created fullgrown, perfect in the image of God;
but as a helpless nursling of animal mind,
as a boy with his mother, unto whom he oweth
more than he ever kenneth or stayeth to think, language,
knowledge, grace, love and those ideal aims whereby   730
his manly intelligence cometh to walk alone.

But how, in this independence and pride, I ask,
how can this younger born stand off so far apart,
clear of all else, that by the mere conscience of things
he can be judge of all and of himself to boot?
For that I find him oftentimes servant and drudge:
as 'tis seen in the true hermeneutic of ART,
whereof all excellence upspringeth of itself,
like a rare fruit upon some gifted stock, ripening
on its arch-personality of inborn faculty,   740
without which gift creativ Reason is barren; altho'
it will collaborate activly and eagerly
with various governance, which appeareth in some
as happy selection and delighted approval
of spiritual nativities, that teem i' the mind,
surging to escape, like to wild bubbles in a pot
when the red fire beneath bristleth, and tortureth
the water to airy ebullience;—or in another
as toilsom evolution of larval germs, which yet
transform while confidently it labŏreth thereat   750
slowly as a modeller in clay. How in its naked self
Reason wer powerless showeth when philosophers
wil treat of Art, the which they are full ready to do,
having good intuition that their master-key
may lie therein: but since they must lack vision of Art

(for elsewise they had been artists, not philosophers)
they miss the way; and ev'n the Greeks themselves, supreme
in making as in thinking, never of their own art
found the true hermeneutick; and the first insight
of the twin-gifted Plato was to Aristotle 760
a crude offence; for Plato said that earthly things,
whether material objects or abstract notions,
wer shadows of Ideas laid up in God's house,
—a dainty dish for the sophistic banqueters.
And yet this delicat doctrin, that held no shield
to Zeno's lancing logic, took not hurt at heart
from any mortal assault, but liveth in the schools
with flourish'd head serene, high and invulnerable;—
because the absurdity of indefinable forms
is less than the denial of existence to thought: 770
and truly if all existence is expression of Mind,
ideas must themselves be truer existences
than whatever else, and in such thought their nearest name.

Powers unseen and unknown are the fountains of life:
no animal but kenneth that sunlight is warm;
no dog but shifteth posture with the shifting shade
reasonably as we: but man maketh a dial for it
to measur his day, and by his abstract intellect

hath taken it for the source and very cause of life

then by science unraveling its physical rays 780

he hath separated some, and found some properties;

but of the whole he knoweth that his analysis

hath not approach'd the secret of their living power.

Nor hath man ever a doubt that mere objects of sense

affect his mental states, nor that the mind in turn

promoteth the action and function of his animal life

in its organs and bones. The Greek astronomer,

gazing with naked eye into the starry night,

forgat his science and, in transport of spirit,

his mortal lot. Then seem'd it to him as if his feet 790

touch'd earth no longer: ἀλλὰ παρ' αὐτῷ Ζανί,

said he, in the treasur'd words that keep his joy from death,

θεοτρεφέος πίμπλαμαι ἀμβροσίης.

Now this imagination of awe and ecstasy,

being proper and common in Man, and where lacking or dull

so ready to suggestion, it seemeth as tho' the eye

had some spiritual vision—as if the idea of Space

and also of God existed in the midnight skies;

and thus men came to think that their corporeal sense

encounter'd rëality in the appearance of things; 800

and, stirr'd by influences that outreaching Reason

kindled unknown desires, their awed souls fell to prayer

(71)

that the great Maker of All would reveal his Being.

If so be then that Reason, our teacher in all the schools,
owneth to existences beyond its grasp, whereon
its richer faculties depend, and that those powers
are ever present influencing the unconscious mind
in its native function to inspire the Will, 'twould seem
that as the waken'd mind fashion'd to'ard intellect
so the dark workings of his animal instincts   810
faced in a new perspectiv to'ard spiritual sight;
and thus man's trouble came of their divergency.
For spiritual perception vague and uncontroll'd
being independent of the abstract intelligence,
he is disconcerted twixt their rival promises,
and, doubtful of his road, he wavereth following
now one now the other: and thus I stand where I conclude
that man's true wisdom were a reason'd harmony
and correlation of these divergent faculties:
this wer the bridge which all men who can see the abyss   820
hav reasonably and instinctivly desired to build;
and all their sacraments and mysteries whatsoe'er
attempt to build it; from devout Pythagoras
to th' last psychologist of Nancy or of Vienna.

And between spiritual emotion and sensuous form
the same living compact maketh our Art, wherein

material appearances engage the soul's depth;
and if in men untrain'd without habit of thought
the ear is more æsthetic than the eye is, this cometh
from thatt sense being the earlier endow'd in animals   830
who, tho' they be all vacant in a picture-gallery
nor see themselves in a mirror, attend to music
and yield to fascination or vague wonder thereat.
So if we, changing Plato's old difficult term,
should rename his Ideas Influences, ther is none
would miss his meaning nor, by nebulous logic,
wish to refute his doctrin that indeed ther are
eternal Essences that exist in themselves,
supreme efficient causes of the thoughts of men.

What is Beauty? saith my sufferings then.—I answer   840
the lover and poet in my loose alexandrines:
Beauty is the highest of all these occult influences,
the quality of appearances that thru' the sense
wakeneth spiritual emotion in the mind of man:
And Art, as it createth new forms of beauty,
awakeneth new ideas that advance the spirit
in the life of Reason to the wisdom of God.
But highest Art must be rare as nativ faculty is

(73)

and her surprise of magic winneth favor of men

more than her inspiration : most are led away   850

by fairseeming pretences, which being wrought for gain

pursue the ephemeral fashion that assureth it;

and their thin influences are of the same low grade

as the unaccomplish'd forms; their poverty is exposed

when they would stake their charm on ethic excellence;

for then weak simulations of virtues appear,

such as convention approveth, but not Virtue itself,

tho' not void of all good : and (as I read) 'twas this

that Benvenuto intended, saying that not only

Virtue was memorable but things so truly done   860

that they wer like to Virtue; and thus prefaced his book,

thinking to justify both himself and his works.

The authority of Reason therefor relieth at last

hereon—that her discernment of spiritual things,

the ideas of Beauty, is her conscience of instinct

upgrown in her (as she unto conscience of all

upgrew from lower to higher) to conscience of Beauty

judging itself by its own beauteous judgment.

And of War she would say : it ranketh with those things

that are like unto virtue, but not virtue itself: 870

rather, in the conscience of spiritual beauty, a vice

that needeth expert horsemanship to curb, yet being

(74)

nativ in the sinew of selfhood, the life of things,

the pride of animals, and virtue of savagery,

so long as men be savage such it remaineth;

and mid the smoke and gas of its new armoury

still, with its tatter'd colours and gilt swords of state,

retaineth its old glory untarnish'd—heroism,

self-sacrifice, disciplin, and those hardy virtues

of courage honour'd in Brasidas, without which   880

man's personality wer meaner than the brutes.

Who hath not known this pictur?—on a hot afternoon

of our high summer in August at the country-seat

of some vext politician, if in their flashing cars

the county-folk gather to his holiday garden,

where for their entertainment he hath outspredd the lawns

with tents and furnish'd tables, flags and tennis-nets,—

if haply he hav set up to dignify his grounds

a classic statue of marble, fetch'd by ship from Greece,

that standeth there in true ideal nakedness   890

mid parasols and silks, how with blank shadow'd eyes

it looketh off from all those aimless idlers there

that flaunt around, now and again blurting perchance

a shamefast shallow tribute to its beauteous presence!

—'tis very like among common concourse of men,

who twixt care of comfort and zeal in worldly affairs
hav proved serving two masters the vanity of both,
when a true soldier appeareth, one compact at heart
of sterner virtues and modesty of maintenance,
mute witness and martyr of spiritual faith, a man   900
ready at call to render his life to keep his soul.

    All *virtue is in her shape so lovely*, that at sight
her lover is enamour'd even of her nativ face.
And here I part from Aristotle, agreeing else
that a good disposition is Goddes happiest gift,
without which, as he addeth, Virtue is unteachable,
but in minds well-disposed may be by Reason upbuilt:
"no man cometh (said she) unto WISDOM but by me";
But when he would exalt this guiding principle
to be thatt part whereby we are in likeness with God,   910
whose Being (saith he) lieth in the unbroken exercise
of absolute intellect—which for their happiness
mankind should strive to attain—I halt thereat: and this
marreth my full accord where, in a famous text
he hath made Desire to be the Prime Mover of all:
because the arch-thinker's heav'n cannot move my desire,
nor doth his pensiv Deity make call on my love.
I see the emotion of saints, lovers and poets all
to be the kindling of some Personality

by an eternizing passion; and that God's worshipper   920
looking on any beauty falleth straightway in love;
and thatt love is a fire in whose devouring flames
all earthly ills are consumed, and at least flash of it,
be it only a faint radiancy, the freed soul glimpseth,
nay ev'n may think to hav felt, some initiat foretaste
of thatt mystic rapture, the consummation of which
is the absorption of Selfhood in the Being of God.

Ideas and influences spiritually discern'd
are of their essence pure: but in the lot of man
nothing is wholly pure; yet all hindrance to good   930
—be good and evil two in love or one in strife—
maketh occasion for it, by contrast heightening,
by challenge and revelly arousing Virtue to act.
Hence 'twill not be with men only of contention and hate,
nor only with the ambitious and disorderly
that combat findeth favor; honest men good and true
who seek peace and ensue it, seeing war as the field
for exercise of spirit that else might fust unused,
embrace the good, and cavil not the inherent terms,
rather welcoming hardship; which by affraying cowards   940
purgeth heroic ranks: and battle rallieth all

keen-hearted sportsmen and the brave gamesters of life,
adventurers whose joy danceth on peril's edge,
for whom life hath no relish save in danger of death;
who love sport for its hazard, and of all their sports
where hazard is at highest look to find the best
there on the field where hourly they may stake their all.
And 'tis because they feel their spirit's ecstasy
is owing in nought to Reason, but exultantly
blendeth with the old Selfhood wherefrom it sprang—'tis thus
they can be friendly at heart with nature's heartlessness,   951
nor heed the wrongs and cruelties that come and pass,
overlook'd as by men who hav suffer'd not nor seen.

But we who hav seen, condemn'd in savage self-defence
to train our peaceful folk in the instruments of death,
and of massacre and mourning hav suffer'd four years—
we hav no need to recount in vindication of peace,
sorrows which no glory of heroism can atone,
horrors which to forget wer cowardice and wrong,
dishonesty of heart and repudiation of soul,—   960
yet gladly might forget in the passing of pain;
and memory is so complacent that we well may fear
lest our children forget;—and see Natur already,
regardless how her fractious babe had scratch'd her cheek,

hath with her showy Invincibles retaken amain
the trenches, and reclothed the devastated lands.

See with how placid mien Athena unhelmeted
rëentering hath possess'd her desolated halls;
how her musical temples and grave schools are throng'd
with fresh youth eager as ever with the old books and games,
their live abounding mirth rëechoing from the walls,   971
where among antique monuments their brothers' names
in long death-roll await the mellowing touch of time.

And why not we forget? How is 't that we dare not
wish to forget and cut this canker of memory
from us, as men diseased in one part of their flesh
find health in mutilation: as if our agony
wer a boon to keep, when in its own happy riddance
'twould die off in the natural oblivion of things,
and with our follies fade: so, each one for himself   980
disbanding his self-share, Reason would dissipate
its own delusion, and lay that spectre of our dismay,
the accumulation of griefs; to which War hath no right
prior or prerogative: miseries lay as thick
and horrors worse when Plague invaded the cities,
Athens or London, raging with polluted flood
in every house, and with revolting torture rack'd
the folk to loathsom deaths; nor men kenn'd as they fell,

desperatly unrepentant to the "scourge of God",

how 'twas the crowded foulness of their own bodies 990

punish'd them so:—alas then in what plight are we,

knowing 'twas mankind's crowded uncleanness of soul

that brought our plague! which yet we coud not cure nor stay;

for Reason had lost control of his hot-temper'd steed

and taken himself infection of the wild brute's madness;

so when its fire slacken'd and the fierce fight wore out,

our fever'd pulse show'd no sober return of health.

Amid the flimsy joy of the uproarious city

my spirit on those first jubilant days of armistice

was heavier within me, and felt a profounder fear 1000

than ever it knew in all the War's darkest dismay.

THE TESTAMENT

OF BEAUTY

BOOK III

Breed

HAVING told of SELFHOOD, ere now I tell of BREED
the younger of the two Arch-Instincts of man's nature,
'twer well here to remember how these pictured steeds
are Ideas construed by the abstract Intellect.

  Whatever abode Philosophy thinketh to build,
to erect a lofty temple that may shrine her faith,
crowning the unvisited holiness of the hills,
or thrust her fair façade amid the noisy dens
of swarming Industry, to invite the sons of toil,
all altitude expanse or grandeur of building   10

subsisteth on foundations buried out of sight,

which yet the good architect carrieth ever in mind,

and keepeth the draft by him stored in his folios.

So herein 'twas laid down what footing Reason plann'd;—

divining Purpose in Natur, it abstracted first

her main intentions, and subsumeth under each

the old animal passions ancillary thereto,

tho' in Nature's economy the same impulse

may work to divers ends, as demonstrably is seen

in the appetite of hunger, which prime in selfhood   20

promoteth no less all living activities,

so universal that some thinkers would make it

a corner-stone, and mixing other like fabric

build thereon confidently, albeit for such deep trust

unfit, being in itself a thing of no substance.

    And truly PLEASUR IN FOOD, common to all animals

that can feel pleasure, comforting the incessant toil

of sustenance to enable their blind energies,

when once it findeth conscience in the Reason of man

is posited by folly as an end-in-itself;   30

til by sensuous refinement it usurpeth rank

beside his intellectual and spiritual joys,—

a road whereon the brutes already had broken ground

(trespassing somewhat haply on nature's allotments),

for a Tyger, when once he hath tasted human flesh,
in pursuit of his prey is more dangerous to men
and chooseth daintily among them; like those cannibals
who yet, for all their courtesy (so travelers tell)
and Spartan stoicism, gaily devour their kind.

From the terrifying jungle of his haunted childhood   40
where prehistoric horror stil lurketh untamed,
man by slow steps withdrew, and from supply of need
fell to pursuit of pleasur, untill his luxury
supplanting brutality invented a new shame;
for with civilization a caste of cooks was bred,
not specialized in structure—as with bees or ants—
but serviceable of either sex and disciplin'd
in such cultur'd tradition that the grammar of it
would stock a library; nor are their banquets spredd
to please the palate only; the eye is invited   50
by dainty disguises and the nostril with scents,
nay ev'n the ear is fed, and on the gather'd guests
a trifling music playeth, dispelling all thought,
that while they fill the belly, the empty mind may float
lightly in the full moonshine of o'erblown affluence.
Thus, when in London city a Guild of merchants dine,
one dinner's cost would ease a whole bye-street of want,

its broken meats outface Christ's thrifty miracle.

But tho' of its mere sensual smirch the scene be cleansed
at fashionable tables, where delicat guests   60
sit and play with their food inattentively, as 'twer
in their relaxation an accidental relish
to the intellectual banter and familiar discourse
of social entertainment—a thing overlook'd
among the agreeable superfluities of life,
trifles good in themselves, and no more censurable
than the fine linen of Ulysses and the brooch
that Penelope gave him, nor the rangled shroud
that she wove for his sire, nor any work of price
that humbly doeth honor unto any temple of God—   70
yet this amenity of Mammon is to the epicure
mere disgust, a farrago of incongruous kickshaws,
a hazardous pampering, as barbarously remote

from pleasure's goal as pothouse cheese and ale.
For Reason once engaged on the æsthetic of food
refineth every means, as those painters in oil
who all their sunless days sat labouring to attain
a chiaroscuro of full colour—so the epicure;
nor planneth he his creation with a less regard
to grandiose composition, in a scheme of morsels   80
gradated to provoke and stimulate alike

digestion and appetite; and each viand married
with a congenial wine, and each wine in itself
a sublimation of fancy, a radiant riotous juice,
and of such priceless rarity as no man can come
but by luck and genius to possess such bottles.

And here the Voluptuary may think his anchor
hath bitten on truth; for surely nothing in nature
fulfilleth more various expectancies of sense
than his wine doth; to the eye luminous as rich gems   90
engendering thru' long æons in the bowels of earth;
to the nostrils reminiscent as subtle odours
of timorous wind-wavering flowers; to the taste
beyond all savours ravishing, insatiable,
yet wholesome as is the incense of forested pines,
when neath their scorching screens they fume the slumberous air;
and to the mind exhilarating, expelling care,
even as those well-toned viols, matured by time, which once,
when the Muse visited Italy to prepare
a voice of beauty for the joy of her children,   100
wer fashion'd by Amati and Stradivari and still,
treasured in their mellow shapelinesses, fulfil
the genius of her omnipotent destiny,—
speaking with incantation of strange magic to charm
the dreams that yet undreamt lurk in the unfathom'd deep

of mind, unfeatur'd hopes and loves and dim desires,
  uttermost forms of all things that shall be.
'Tis thus by the live firework of his wine allured
that the epicure thinketh he hath wherewithal to pave
thru' palate and gullet a right path for his soul,   110
each feast as a symphonic poem, preluding
to melodious Andante Scherzo and final Fugue,—
a microcosm, as those musical pæans are
  that perish not in the using, but persist
strengthening their immortality while millions feed
on their unquenchable loveliness evermore.
  In such fine artistry of his putrefying pleasures
he indulgeth richly his time untill the sad day come
when he retireth with stomach Emeritus
to ruminate the best devour'd moments of life;   120
like any old fox-hunter his good days with the hounds,
any angler or cricketer, for he too hath follow'd
his sport to himself, and each good day of sport (and thatt
the dog knoweth and enjoyeth with his Master as well)
is a thing in itself, whole even as life is one.
  This is the supreme ecstasy of the mountaineer,
to whom the morn is bright, when with his goal in sight,
some icepeak high i' the heav'ns, he is soul-bounden for it,
prospecting the uncertain clue of his perilous step

to scale precipices where no foot clomb afore,   130
for good or ill success to his last limit of strength;
his joy in the doing and his life in his hand
he glorieth in the fortunes of his venturous day;
'mid the high mountain silences, where Poesy
lieth in dream and with *the secret strength of things*
that governs thought inhabiteth, where man wandereth
into God's presence:—But what heav'nly or earthly Muse
attendeth the epicure? Nay, what man deigneth ear
to his grovelling tale? His gluttony rotteth and stinketh
in the dust-bin of Ethick.—Howso thatt may be,   140
the thing cometh of Self, as War doth; and hereby
'twer well to note how some would derive War from Breed,
tho' sex is but the occasion, when jealousy of love
provoketh Selfhood to anger: indeed Herodotus,
seeking the root-cause of the implacable enmity
'twixt Hellenes and Asiatics to convey his book,
dresseth up a frontispiece of four royal rapes,
of Io and Medea, Europa and Helen of Troy,
playing no doubt upon the flair of his hearers,
who love him stil for his good faith in his fables.   150

YET our distinction is proper and holdeth fast. Now BREED

is to the race as SELFHOOD to the individual;
and these two prime Instincts as they differ in purpose
are independent each from other, and separat
as are the organic tracts in the animal body
whereby they function; and tho' Breed is needful alike
to plants as to animals, yet its apparatus
is found in animals of a more special kind;
and since race-propagation might hav been assured
without differentiation of sex, we are left to guess   160
nature's intention from its full effects in man:
and such matter is the first that wil follow hereon.

Remembering my dissension from Spinoza here,
I think of him, Bruno's pupil, ὑψίπολις
ἄπολις, in his pride at his bench intently
shaping his lenses, and how he in thatt irksome toil
to earn his bread, the while he ponder'd his great book,
was perfecting the tool that invited science
to ever minuter anatomy, untill she took skill
to handle invisibles; and lately upon thatt path   170
hath divined, in the observed fertilization of plants,
atomic mechanism with unlimited power
to vary the offspring in character, by mutual
inexhaustible interchange of transmitted genes;

a theory on such wide experiment upbuilt
that the enrichment of species may be assumed to be
the purpose of natur in the segregation of sex.
Yet this new knowledge throweth no light on our way
to a purposeful and wise selfbreeding of mankind
which, coud it be, would then responsibly overrule   180
all indiscriminat mating: tho' from such ordeal
our hybrid wisdom well might shrink: rather we see
complexity irresoluble in obscurity:
So may we stil follow our instinctiv preferences
unrebuked, and in love of Beauty affirm our faith
that our happiest espousals are nature's free gift.

   And the origin of sex lieth yet in thatt darkness
where all origins are—since definition of links
within our causal chain advanceth us no way
in sensible approachment to the first Cause of all: 190
we are happy in our discoveries as a child thinketh
he is nearer to the Pole-star when he is put to bed:
yet, tracing backwards in the story of sex, the steps
of our carpeted staircase are familiar and strong.

   First among lowest types of life we think to find
no separation of sex: plants in the next degree
show differentiation at puberty with some signs
of mutual approachment: next in higher animals

an early differentiation, and at puberty
periodic appetite with mutual attraction   200
sometimes engaging Beauty: then at last in man
all these same characters promoted and strengthen'd
to a constant conscient passion, by Reason transform'd
to'ard altruistic emotion and spiritual love.

Breed then together with Selfhood steppeth in pair,
for as Self grew thru' Reason from animal rage
to vice of war and gluttony, but meanwhile uprose
thru' motherly yearning to a profounder affection,
so Breed, from like degrading brutality at heart,
distilleth in the altruism of spiritual love   210
to be the sublimest passion of humanity,
with parallel corruption; in its supremacy
confess'd of all, since all in their degree hav felt
its divine exaltation and bestial abasement.
It hath sanctified fools and degraded heroes;
and tho' the warrior wil lightly leave his lady
to join in battle (so the weight of the elder horse
side-wrencheth at the yoke), he wil return to her
more gladly, and often rue his infidelity.

In higher natures, poetic or mystical,   220
sense is transfigur'd quite; as once with Dante it was

who saw the grace of a fair Florentine damsel
as WISDOM UNCREATE: for it happen'd to him
in thatt awakening miracle of Love at first sight,
which is to many a man his only miracle,
his one divine Vision, his one remember'd dream—
it happ'd to Dante, I say, as with no other man
in the height of his vision and for his faith therein:
the starry plenitude of his radiant soul,
searching for tenement in the bounties of life,   230
encounter'd an aspect of spiritual beauty
at the still hour of dawn which is holier than day:
as when a rose-bud first untrammeleth the shells
of her swathing petals and looseneth their embrace,
so the sunlight may enter to flush the casket
of her virgin promise, fairer than her full bloom
shall ever be, ere its glories lie squander'd in death:—
'Twas of thatt silent meeting his high vision came
rapturous as any vision ever to poet giv'n;
since in thatt Sacrament he rebaptized his soul   240
and lived thereafter in Love, by the merit of Faith
toiling to endow the world: and on those feather'd wings
his mighty poem mounted panting, and lieth now
with all its earthly tangle by the throne of God.
    So to Lucretius also seeking Order in Chance

some frenzy of Beauty came, neath which constraint he left

his atoms in the lurch and fell to worshipping

Aphroditè, the naked Goddess of man's breed;

and waving the oriflamme of her divinity

above the march of his slow-trooping argument,　　　　250

he attributeth to her the creation and being

of all Beauty soe'er: NEC SINE TE QUICQUAM

DIAS IN LUMINIS ORAS EXORITUR,

NEQUE FIT LAETUM NEQUE AMABILE QUICQUAM.

So well did he in his rapture: such is Beauty's power

physical or spiritual; and if it be the cause

of spiritual emotion (as hath been said), 'tis plain

that Beauty wil be engaged in man's love, in so far

as 'tis a proper and actual attribute of man:

first, as in animals, of his physical form,　　　　260

to which, when beauty of soul is added, the addition

but marketh more specially its human character.

　　Thus Shakespeare, *in the sessions of sweet silent thought*

gathering from memory the idealization of love,

when he launch'd from their dream-sheds those golden sonnets

that swim like gondolas i' the wake of his drama,

fashion'd for their ensignry a pregnant axiom,

and wrote: *From fairest creatures we desire increase*

That thereby Beauty's Rose might never die; wherein

he asserteth beauty to be of love the one motiv,   270
and thatt in double meaning of object and cause.

And tho' blind instinct wer full puissant of itself
for propagation of man, yet the attraction of beauty
bettereth the species, nor without it coud ther hav been
effect in spirit; and that the poet guarded this
showeth in his lyric, where of Sylvia 'tis enquired
why all the swaïns commend her, and he replyeth thereto
Holy fair and wïse ïs she, thus giving to Soul
first place, thereafter to Body and last of the trine
Intelligence; and thatt is their right order in Love.   280

And this high beauty of spirit—in the conscience of it,
in the love of it, and the appearances of it—
tho' it hav no quarrel with thatt physical beauty
whereof 'twas born, when once 'tis waken'd in the mind
needeth no more support of the old animal lure,
but absolute in its transmitted power and grace
maketh a new beauty of its own appearances.

Thus oft the full majesty and happiness of love
is found in lovers whose corporeal presences
would seem disloyalty to the gay worshippers   290
of the goddess of grace, nor fit to approach her shrine:
yet lightly wil Love rate the ridicule of them
whose passion, subsisting in the flourish of flesh,

outlasteth not its brief prime, but must fade and fade
as thatt fadeth, and when it perisheth perish;
and who themselves—save in the rout of their revel
they hav perish'd immature—provide tales of despair,
disease and madness; melancholy tragedies
of ignobility unredeem'd, to scare mankind.

But love's true passion is of immortal happiness,   300
whereof the Greeks, maybe,—whose later poets told
of a heav'nly Aphroditè—had some dim prescience
before man ever arrived at thatt wisdom thru' Christ,
and now teacheth to his children as their birthright,—a gift
whose wealth is amplified by spending, and its charm
rejuvenated by habit, that dulleth all else:
nor needeth it for joy to look off from this earth
and beyond, nor to sit on the schoolbench with them
who dispute in argument the existence of God;
being of eternity it overcometh evil   310
as any nativ disposition is apt to do,
but more surely and with its virtue more self-secure
than the merry or sad heart is, that in laughter or tears
wil keep unchanged its temper, whatsoe'er befall;
  so priketh hem Nature in hir corages.
But think not Aphroditè therefor disesteem'd

for rout of her worshippers, nor sensuous Beauty
torn from her royal throne, who is herself mother
of heav'nly Love (so far as in human aspect
eternal essence can hav mortal parentage),   320
our true compass in art as our comfort in faith,
our daily bread of pleasur;—enough that thus I deem
of Beauty among Goddes best gifts, and even above
   the pleasur of Virtue accord it honour of men.

   The allure of bodily beauty is mutual in mankind
as is the instinct of breed, which tho' it seem i' the male
more activ, is i' the female more predominant,
more deeply engaging life, grave and responsible.
Thus while in either sex celibat lives are led
without impoverishment of intellect or will,   330
this thing is rare in women, whereas in the man
virginity may seem a virile energy
in its angelic liberty, prerequisit
to the perfection of some high personality.
   And here we are driv'n to enquire of Reason how it came
that bodily beauty is deem'd a feminin attribute,
since not by science nor æsthetick coud we arrive
at such a judgment. But not triflingly to trench

on prehistoric problems, 'twil be enough to say

that from the first it may not always hav been so,   340

and primacy of beauty may hav once lain with the male,

in days of pagan savagery, afore men left

their hunting and took tillage of the fields in hand,

superseding the women and all their moon-magic,

to invent a reason'd labor of intensiv culture,

as now 'tis seen;—whether in remotest orient lands

whose cockcrow is our curfew, where Chineses swarm

teasing their narrow plots with hand and hoe, carrying

their own dung on their heads obsequiously as ants;

or on our western farms where now machines usurp   350

such manual labor, and hav with their strange forms dethroned

the heraldry of the seasons, fair emblems of eld

that seem'd the inalienable imagery of mankinde.

How was November's melancholy endear'd to me

in the effigy of plowteams following and recrossing

patiently the desolat landscape from dawn to dusk,

as the slow-creeping ripple of their single furrow

submerged the sodden litter of summer's festival!

They are fled, those gracious teams; high on the headland now

squatted, a roaring engin toweth to itself   360

a beam of bolted shares, that glideth to and fro

combing the stubbled glebe: and agriculture here,

blotting out with such daub so rich a pictur of grace,
hath lost as much of beauty as it hath saved in toil.

Again where reapers, bending to the ripen'd corn,
were wont to scythe in rank and step with measured stroke,
a shark-tooth'd chariot rampeth biting a broad way,
and, jerking its high swindging arms around in the air,
swoopeth the swath. Yet this queer Pterodactyl is well,
that in the sinister torpor of the blazing day   370
clicketeth in heartless mockery of swoon and sweat,
as 'twer the salamandrine voice of all parch'd things:
and the dry grasshopper wondering knoweth his God.

Or what man feeleth not a new poetry of toil,
whenas on frosty evenings neath its clouding smoke
the engin hath huddled-up its clumsy threshing-coach
against the ricks, wherefrom laborers standing aloft
toss the sheaves on its tongue; while the grain runneth out,
and in the whirr of its multitudinous hurry
it hummeth like the bee, a warm industrious boom   380
that comforteth the farm, and spreadeth far afield
with throbbing power; as when in a cathedral awhile
the great diapason speaketh, and the painted saints
feel their glass canopies flutter in the heav'nward prayer.

Thus hath man's Reason dealt since he took spade in hand,

either by wit of the insect or of the engineer:
and they who hav come to think that in remotest times
Eve delved and Adam span, can show matriarchy of sorts
had precedent in natur, ostensibly among birds,
whose males more gaudily feather'd wil disport their charms
and dance in coquetry to win the admiring hens: 391
Verily it well may be that sense of beauty came
to those primitiv bipeds earlier than to man.

  But howso in patriarchal times our code upgrew,
it hath decretals honour'd in the courts of Love:
'tis the faith of all poets from the Troubadours
to Shelley's broken amours, and that the fair Muses
should hav masculin wooers was Apollo's will
who favour'd his own sex. But had the god inspired
poetesses many as poets—coud thatt hav been—   400
follies had cancel'd out truly in the equation of love,
and steadier fire of passion would hav warm'd the world.
Today if any lady in her boudoir rhymeth,
she is drown'd in man's tradition and disguiseth her tone,
transposing her high music to the lower clef;
or deemeth thatt the orthodoxy of the sapphic mode,
because of the two love songs which pedantry hath saved
of Sappho's complisht artistry, one by mischance,
in thatt muliebrous dump which gave Catullus pause,

hath this falsification of her true soprano.   410
But 'twas the deeper voice that robed passion in song,
with the masculin emotion that glorify'd it:
and man, finding elation in physical beauty
and in the passion of sex his chief transport of soul,
ascribed supremacy of beauty to woman's grace,
and she to'ardly accepted his idolatry.
Yet if the passion had been identic in the twain,
the woman surely had found her like ideal in man;
but the motivs of Nature that determin life
are hidden, and with the sexes they are unlike in love.   420
    For tho' true loves are mutual and of equal strength
and their bodily communion is a sacrament—
like those irrevocable initiations of yore
whose occult ritual it was profane to disclose—
and in its uttermost surrender of secrecies
hallowing brute instinct, symbolizeth approach
to satisfaction of unattainable desire;
yet in fullest devotion and frankest abandon
of eager and mutual mating, whether or no she ken,
the woman's choice hath been by a deeper purpose led,   430
whereof the mastering revelation awaiteth her
in the reality of her Motherhood; wherefor,
that her son may be noble, she wil seek his sire

where her ideal, howe'er vaguely imagin'd, lieth
outside her sphere, beyond her—and so thinketh she less
of thatt for which her mate praiseth and seeketh her,
and longing evermore for what she most lacketh,
in her thought of wisdom looketh for higher things,
and for immortal Roses desireth increase.

How Natur (as Plato saith) teacheth man by beauty,   440
and by the lure of sense leadeth him ever upward
to heav'nly things, and how the mere sensible forms
which first arrest him take-on ever more and more
spiritual aspect,—yet discard not nor disown
their sensuous beauty, since thatt is eternal and sure,
the essence thereof being the reverent joy of life—
this everywhere is seen and most overtly in Breed
(too many in truth ther be who find it never elsewhere);
yet man is slow to see that love's call to woman
is graver and more solemn than it can be to him,   450
by reason of her higher function and duty therein,
and that all past attainment which his spirit hath won
came to him thru' motherhood of the nursling boy;—
yea, ev'n the dignity of his masculin intellect,
that outreacheth her range, was first of her making
and never coud hav fruited but for the devout

fostering environment of her lovingkindness:
nor can man's futur attainment forgo thatt shelter,
wherewith her precocious girlhood accompanieth
the evergrowing incumbency of his pupillage,   460
as it grew in the brutes: .. and here 'tis seen again
how 'tis a backsliding and treason against nature
when women wil unsex their own ideal of Love,
and ignorantly aiming to be in all things as men,
would make love as men make it—tho' Sappho did thatt,
who rare among women for manly mastery of art,
a Nonsuch of her kind, exceeded by default,
nondescript, and for lack of the true feminin
borrow'd effeminacy of men, the incontinents,
who, ranking with gluttons in Aristotle's book,   470
made a lascivious pleasure of their Lesbian loves;
till in the event the euphony of her isle's fair name
whisper'd an unspoken and else unspeakable shame.

    Nor can the ethic that here intrudeth be deny'd,
since if men speak of morals 'tis of sex they think;
forwhy the passion of it both transporteth their souls
and troubleth daily life with problems of conduct.

    Now to the most who are like to read my English poem
christian marriage wil seem a stablish'd ordinance

as universal, wholesome and needful to man   480

as WHEAT is, which, ubiquitous, and sib to a weed

that yet wil hamper its cultur, overruleth all else,

weigheth our gold by single grains, and harvested

measureth in sacks the peace and welfare of the world,

our BREAD OF LIFE, and symbol of the food of the soul.

But tho' monogamy had been by wise lawgivers

coded with rights and duties and property, and thus

by Jewish use or Roman held place in the Church,

the instinct of sex was ever anathema to the Essenes

whose thought handsel'd the faith; 'twas to thatt sect the accurst

contamination of all spiritual purity: 491

and only after tough battle against two mighty outbursts

of Pagan Poetry coud marriage come in the end

to its own, from being a tolerated discordancy

to be an accepted harmony, and hallow'd as such

within the Church, a sacrament. Of those two wars

the story is long, and now 'tis here briefly to tell.

The first War of the Essenes was with the poetry

of SELFHOOD, those sagas and epic rhapsodies

which had burst forth to flood all Europe in the time   500

of the northern invasions, when the hideous Huns,

extending the right wing of their havoc, swept down
on the old land of the Goths. Soon as their arrows prick'd
our Teuton forefathers, a clash of arms and yell
of battle arose, that in the unsearchable storage
of earth's high firmament vibrateth to this day.

    The warriors, who in vain defence of home escaped
the first mauling and massacre, wer driven forth
and, pressing Westward desperatly, became in turn
themselves ruthless invaders, live firebrands that spredd   510
the blast of their contagion to Allemand and Frank,
Burgundian, Vandal and Lombard, from Angle and Dane
to furthest Kelt; and with the sword follow'd the song,
an inextinguishable pæan of battle and blood.

    A sudden eruption of nature, as when earth quaketh
and faltering along the edges of its wrinkling shell
the mountains roar and crack, and vent their ruddy bowels
in spume of molten lava; as oft hath been where now
some gracious valley embosom'd in soft azurous hills
smileth, an Eden as fair as Goddes love was feign'd   520
to have planted for man's use—thatt lost garden regain'd,
lost once thru' pride and now by long stooping regain'd,—
a pictur and outward symbol of the comfort of them
whose spirits dwell in the Eden that the Muse hath made
her garden of soul in *the golden lapses of Time*;

and if, tracing to its source some Heliconian rill,
its mossgrown cave is found in the black splinter'd rock,
where thatt once cool'd and stay'd, a volcanic moraine
to bank his blossom'd Paradise and feed his vines,
ther-after to the poet all his joy wil seem   530
a strange mysterious dream, a thread of beauty eterne
enwoven in mortal change, and he himself a flower
fertilized awhile on the quench'd torrent of Hell.

Now when Rome's mitred prelates ambled o'er the Alps
to hold the Gallic provinces, whose overlords
their missioners had won to the confession of Christ,
the pagan folk submissiv to constraint wer driv'n
in flocks to th' font, but got little washing therein.
   Whatever of kindliness Tacitus once had found
sequester'd in the rude homesteads of Germany   540
was burnt up in thatt fiery ordeal, which taught them
the joy of frenzy and prowess, and the songs whereby
they glorify'd the memory of successful lust,
and stirr'd anew the fierce delight of battle and blood.
   A wilder strain maybe than the lost Bedouin songs,
that seal'd the weird which the Angel in Araby foretold
to the outcast bondwoman in the famishing desert,
and she to her son,—that his horoscope was to range

like the wild ass untameable, and his hand should be
'gainst ev'ry man, and ev'ry man's hand against him.   550
   Wherefor hitting for remedy on Plato's old plan,
when he proscribed Homer from his Utopian schools—
saying that morals wer unteachable to men
who imputed mortal passions to the immortal gods—,
the priests denounced the bards, and would hav stopp'd their mouths;
but finding that forbiddance met with no regard
they turn'd to assure their flock by amity, and to comb
the fleece they might not shear: upon which way they wrought
some mitigation, and growing reconciled to the art,
and grudging to the heathen what might serve the Church,   560
they took thought to divert it, and engaged the bards
to make like stirring balladry of the Bible tales:
wherein, joining themselves with good heart to the work,
their first grains of allowance multiply'd to pounds;
while with their clerkly skill they sat fast to transcribe
the old pagan tales, redacted to the amended form
in which we know them, with what other numberless
wonder-lives of the Saints they wrote, symbolic masques
of Christian orthodoxy, and later mystery-plays.
   So all these diverse stuffs thru' the dark centuries   570
lay quietly a-soak together in the dye-vats, wherein
our British Arthur was clandestinly christen'd

and crown'd, and all his knights cleansed and respirited,
reclothed as might be: for the dispossess'd devils
had kindly accepted their rebate, content to find
their old home swept and garnish'd; and tho' verily
in their domestication, as 'tis with brutes, they had lost
keenness of sense and true compact of character,
they flourish to this day the darlings of our poets,
who drape their model Arthur to their taste, whereas   580
time was when good St. Andrew strode forth in plate-mail.

  While thus the Catechists made compromising peace
with the poetry of SELFHOOD, ere the fight was won
in rescue of womanhood from the ravish of war,
a new era had dawn'd and a new strain of song,
the young poetry of BREED; and the conflict therewith
is in my story styled the second Essene War.
  'Twas no Huns now that stirr'd the Frankish heart to sing,
nay rather Athena's call, and the gracious emblems
of Hellenic humanity, that long had drown'd   590
where they had sunk o'erwhelm'd in the wreckage of Rome,
undersuck'd in the wallow, when Cæsar's great ship
founder'd with all its toys decadent in the deep,
now freshly of their buoyancy up-struggling here and there
to ride in sparkling dance on the desolat sea:

Or what grave lore had refuged with the Ishmaelite
was stealing back from exile to its western home,
its mansion of birthright, and had now already inspired
passionat Abelard, who with his ethnic books
was heralding in Paris that full Renaissance   600
which should illumin Europe, and plant her cities
with Universities of learning, sanctuaries
of spirit, our schools of thought and science to this day.

    Full Springtime was not yet surely, nor soon to be:
'twas as mayhap *à ce jour de Saint Valentin*
que chacun doit choisir son per, or a later day
of February, when in the shelter'd woodland
the Sun with broadening smile thinketh to intercalate
a glad red-letter'd feast in Winter's almanac,
which the thrush boldly announceth—tho' the migrant birds
hav yet made no return upon the balmy sprays,   611
but the small homekeepers muster what choir they can:
Not elsewise was thatt first impetuous raid that storm'd
the rear of the dark ages prematurely; and yet
the singers wer so many that man marveleth stil
whence they came, or by what spontaneous impulse sang.

    As well might be with one who wendeth lone his way
beside the watchful dykes of the flat Frisian shore,
what hour the wading tribes, that make their home and breed

numberless on the marshy polders, creep unseen   620
widely dispersed at feed, and silent neath the sun
the low unfeatured landscape seemeth void of life—
when without warning suddenly all the legion'd fowl
rise from their beauties' ambush in the reedy beds,
    and on spredd wings with clamorous ecstasy
carillioning in the air manœuvre, and where they wheel
transport the broken sunlight, shoaling in the sky—
with like sudden animation the fair fields of France
gave birth to myriad poets and singers unknown,
who in a main flight gathering their playful flock   630
settled in Languedoc, on either side the Rhone
within the court and county of Raymond of Toulouse.

   Nor wer these Troubadours hucksters of song who tuned
their pipes for fee: some far glimpse of the heav'nly Muse
had reach'd and drawn the soul by the irresistible
magnet of love: as when in the blockish marble
the sculptor's thought of beauty loometh into shape
neath his rude hammerstrokes, ere the true form is seen;
so had the monks' rough-hewing of the old pagan tales
discover'd virtue:—an Ideal of womanhood   640
had striven into outline; which, tho' passion heeded not
yet art had grasp'd, divining fresh motiv for skill,
whereby knights, churchmen, monks, courtiers and scholars all

childishly wer enthrall'd: ev'n kings found honor in rhyme
whose royalty is today its only honor, and to us
would seem frivolity, knew we not that we watch
beside the rocking-cradle of babes, whose prattling tongues
should oust monarchic Latin from his iron throne—
which not the slaughter of this one innocent coud save:
Skysoarers should be rear'd of such young flutterers;   650
for whom two freaks of fortune happily conspired,
a fine phantasy of spirit with light fabric of art;
so the faint dream of chivalry, as it took-on form,
tripp'd delicatly with the delicat music
of the tentativ language, whose mincing metres
imposed good manners on the articulation of speech.

    While in such play Count Raymond's folk lived joyfully,
Provence seem'd to mankind the one land of delight,—
a country where a man might fairly choose to dwell;
tho' some would rather praise the green languorous isles,   660
Hawaii or Samoa, and some the bright Azores,
Kashmire the garden of Ind, or Syrian Lebanon
and flowery Carmel; or wil vaunt the unstoried names
of African Nairobi, where by Nyanza's lakes
Nile hid his flooding fountain, or in the New World
far Pasadena's roseland, whence who saileth home
westward wil in his kalendar find a twin day.

But I in England starving neath the unbroken glooms
of thatt dreariest November which wrapping the sun,
damping all life, had robb'd my poem of the rays   670
whose wealth so far had sped it, I long'd but to be
i' the sunshine with my history; and the names that held
place in my heart and now shall hav place in my line
wer Avignon, Belcaire, Montélimar, Narbonne,
Béziers, Castelnaudary, Béarn and Carcasonne,
and truly I coud hav shared their fancy coud I hav liv'd
among those glad Jongleurs, living again for me,
and had joy'd with them in thatt liberty and good-will
which men call toleration, a thing so stiff to learn
that to sceptics 'tis left and cynics. In Provence   680
Jew quarrel'd not with Gentile; ther was peace and love
'twixt Saracen and Christian, Catalan and Frank;
and (wonder beyond wonder) here was harbour'd safe,
flourishing and multiplying, thatt sect of all sects
abominable, persecuted and defamed,
who with their Eastern chaffering and insidious talk
had ferreted thru' Europe to find peace on earth
with Raymond of Toulouse,—those ancient Manichees.

Restless and impatient man's mind is ever in quest
of some system or mappemond or safeguard of soul,   690

and coming not at Truth—ev'n as a dry-athirst horse
that drinketh eagerly of the first gilded puddle,—
he espouseth delusion and sweareth fealty thereto:
and since common conditions breed common opinion,
nations lie fascinated in their swaddling clothes
crampt, and atrophied with their infantile suctions.
So in the inmost sanctum of the Hindu mind
a milch-cow is enshrined: but those dour Manichees
wer trifling with no symbols; their wild faith had grown
deep-rooted on the prime obsession of savagery,   700
thatt first terrifying nightmare of dawning conscience
which, seeing in natur a power maleficent to man,
estopp'd his growth in love: for these zealots ascribed
this visible world to the work of a devil,
from all time Goddes foe and enemy to all good:
In hate of which hellpower so worthy of man's defiance
they had lost the old fear, and finding internecine war
declared twixt flesh and spirit in the authentic script
of Paul of Tarsus, him they took for master, and styled
themselves Paulicians the depositaries of Christ.   710

   Their creed—better than other exonerating God
from blame of evil—and their austere asceticism
shamed the half-hearted clerics, whose licence in sin
confirm'd the uncompromising logic, which inferr'd

a visible earthly Church to be Satan's device,
the Pope his minister,—him, the third Innocent,
who held his wide ambition for the will of God,
his fulminating censure for the voice of Christ;
and, troubled now that he coud neither cleanse nor cure,
persuade not nor command, fell; and betray'd by zeal   720
(as angry Peter once to serve Christ with the sword),
preach'd a Crusade within the fold,—thatt bloody wrath
label'd in history The Albigensian war,
a sinking millstone heavy as ever pontiff tied
round the neck of the Church. For the champions of Christ
outdid the heathen Huns in cruelty, and in the end
was Raymond's county ravaged to ruin and his folk
massacred all or burnt alive, man woman and child,
and their language wiped out, so that a man today
reading Provençal song studieth in a dead tongue.   730

Yet many Troubadours escaping from slaughter
fled to the Italian cities where the New Learning
gave kind asylum to their secret flame; and ere
within the Church's precincts they had raised a song,
Chivalry had won acceptance in the ideal of sex
and, blending with the worship of the Mother of God,
assured the consecration of MARRIAGE, still unknown
save to the christian folk of Europe whence it sprang.

Thus, as it came to pass, the second Essene War
brought the New Life in which full soon Dante was born.   740

The motive of Selfhood is common to all Being,
the universal Mind informing existence,
and had ther been no beauty in life nor any joy
beyond thatt ground-pleasure, which all creatures may feel
in the inconscient functionings of their organisms
and satisfaction of instinct—had thatt been, ev'n so
nothing had lack'd to inspire the selfassertion of man:
But since ther is beauty in nature, mankind's love of life
apart from love of beauty is a tale of no count;
and tho' he linger'd long in his forest of fear,   750
or e'er his apprehensiv wonder at unknown power
threw off the first night-terrors of his infant mind,
the vision of beauty awaited him, and step by step
    led him in joy of spirit to full fruition.

Now as with Selfhood so was it again with Breed;
for the fashioning of sex was attended thru'out
by necessary attractions—as 'tis seen in plant
or animal, and these as they suffice in brutes
suffice in man so far as he also is animal;

but being specifically endow'd he must in course   760

hav with the growth of reason outgrown the animal wont;

and in perfection of kind he surely had lost his lure,

had he not learn'd in beauty to transfigure love.

   Many shy at such doctrin: Science, they wil say,

knoweth nought of this beauty. But what kenneth she

of color or sound? Nothing: tho' science measure true

every wave-length of ether or air that reacheth sense,

there the hunt checketh, and her keen hounds are at fault;

for when the waves hav pass'd the gates of ear and eye

all scent is lost: suddenly escaped the visibles   770

are changed to invisible; the fine-measured motions

to immeasurable emotion; the cypher'd fractions

to a living joy that man feeleth to shrive his soul.

How should science find beauty? Leibnitz rightly is held

the most irrefutable of all philosophers,

because he boldly excised the intrinse knot from the rope

and, showing both ends free, proclaim'd no knot had been;

imagining two independent worlds that move

in pre-establish'd harmony twixt matter and mind;

—a pleasant freak of man's godlike intelligence,   780

vex'd by so vain a need; and thinking, with a thought

so inconceivable, to save appearances.

That ther is beauty in natur and that man loveth it
are one thing and the same; neither can be derived
apart as cause of the other: and here it is to tell
how female beauty came to be the common lure
in human marriage.—First in animal mating
the physical attractions, as they evolved with sense,
took-on beautiful forms, til beauty (as in bird-song)
was recognized consciently and exploited by art,   790
and after in man became that ladder of joy whereon
slowly climbing at heaven he shall find peace with God,
and beauty be wholly spiritualised in him,
as in its primal essence it must be conceived.

This ken we truly, that as wonder to intellect,
so for the soul desire of beauty is mover and spring;
whence, in whatever his spirit is most moved, a man
wil most be engaged with beauty; and thus in his "first love"
physical beauty and spiritual are both present
mingled inseparably in his lure: then is he seen   800
in the ecstasy of earthly passion and heav'nly vision
to fall to idolatry of some specious appearance
as if 'twer very incarnation of his heart's desire,
whether eternal and spiritual, as with Dante it was,
or mere sensuous perfection, or as most commonly
a fusion of both—when if distractedly he hav thought

to mate mortally with an eternal essence
all the delinquencies of his high passion ensue.

    Verily if Hope wer not itself a happiness
sorrow would far outweigh our mortal joy, but Hope   810
incarnat in the blood kindleth its hue no less
with every breath, to flood all the sluices of life
long as the heart can beat. And yet in love-mating
hope's ideal is so rich and fulfilment so rare,
that common minds in trudge with common experience
may think to amend their lot by renouncing life-vows,
as a vain bondage perversiv of happiness.

    And coud man separate brutal from spiritual,
and in things of the flesh liv as animals do
stealing their food and seizing the delight of the hour,   820
thatt were reasonable enough and might be wise in man;
but such divorcement being in the provision of things
shut out, ther is no way left nor choice for him, unless
he would make shipwreck, and of mere brutality
fall to pieces—ther is no hope for him but to attune
nature's diversity to a human harmony,
and with faith in his hope and full courage of soul
realizing his will at one with all nature,
devise a spiritual ethick for conduct in life.

    Refusal of christian marriage is, as 'twer in art,   830

to impugn the credit of the most beautiful things
because ther are so few of them, and hold it folly
to aim at excellence where so few can succeed;
and where any success pincheth the happiness
of the far greater number, who left to themselves
might feel fuller content admiring common things
or ugly, and be happier in whatever likings
they can indulge. Altho' they know it not, this is
the humanitarianism of democracy;
and since ther is in the mass little good to look for   840
but what instruction, authority and example impose,
Ethick and Politick alike hav trouble in store.

Now mere impulse of sex,—from animal mating
to the vision of Dante—tho' strong in all degrees,
is not the bond of marriage. Nay, if breeding ceased,—
all motiv to it, liking for it and thought of it,—
women and men would mate; and, whatever might lack,
married life might be found a more congenial state,
and *marriage of true minds* hav less *impediment*.
Happiness, which all seek, is not composable   850
of any summation of particular pleasures;
the happiness in marriage dependeth for-sure
not on the animal functions, but on qualities

of spirit and mind that are correlated therewith.

So 'twas not of false ethick or weak prudery
when thatt old Hebrew poet, in his mighty myth
of man's creation, imagin'd Eve's predestiny
to be helpmate and comfort to God's perfect man;
nor in thatt strange fashioning of her from Adam's rib
fudged he his symbol; perfect man being in thatt theft   860
imperfected by loss of an original part
now personate in Eve, of whom he should require
what was in first design confused in his nature,
and from thatt fleshly cleavage find true tally of flesh.

This myth was law to th' Jew, and 'twas men of their clan
(those same Essenes whose creed prevail'd so long),
who, when Christ's mournful company wer by his death
reft of their earthly dreams, took courage and reset
their disillusion'd hope bolder—to look no more
for Rome and Cæsar's overthrow, but rather expect   870
Jahveh's wrathful dissolution of all creation;
that Christ would rëappear in pitiless Godhead
full suddenly and full soon, to judge the world of sin,
and with his angels gather-up his living elect
to his new Jerusalem, those few Saints undefiled,
who had *wash'd their robes to whiteness in the blood o' the Lamb.*

Now those stern Puritans who liv'd but in thatt faith,

in whom motiv and lure of breed wer wholly extinct,
execrating the body as other men flee death,
had no fear of contamination nor thought of ill   880
in taking women in marriage, each man one to himself,
as comrades indispensable, of spiritual aid.

Truly myths so ancient and examples of life,
fish'd-up out of the old jumble-box of history,
can find but little credit with this generation
who, like to children absorb'd in the scientific toys
of their high-kilted gossips, care not to ransack
the nursery cupboard for their grand-dam's old playthings;
tho' family relics are they, once loved, and may show
how that in man's eternal quest of happiness,   890
contempt of fleshly pleasur is as near to his spirit
as is the love of it to his animal nature.
Vestiges of his stony asceticism imbue
all time, thick as the strewage of his flinty tools,
disseminat wheresoe'er he hath dwelt; nor need we now,
from where they sleep bedded on archæologic shelves,
fetch down upon the lecture-table our specimens
to teach what manners went to the making of man;
having such living witness of harmonized life
in the aristocracy of our English motherhood,   900

whence the nobility of our sons came, and therewith
precedence of their courtesy title in the world;
a tradition of good-faith, humanity and courage,
that year by year flowereth on the grafted stock
of Saxon temperament; the which slow or dead
to beauty, is but a dullard in spiritual sense.

And so the character of our common folk, up-built
in the commanding presence of feminin grace,
won therefrom (as I hold) its vulgar excelence;
for finding their own conduct unconformable   910
to beauty of so high grade, they guarded it apart
submissiv in its own status, a kindly thing
with nativ honesty and good commonsense convinced;
and, easing embarrassment with the humour of life,
paid due respect and honour where they felt 'twas due,
so they might goodtemper'dly and in laughable wise
hobnob with ugliness, and jest at frightfulness,
and keep the farce up mirthfully in the face of death.
If any see not this fractur in our midst, because
the pieces are in place, 'tis pictured for him true   920
in Shakespeare's drama, where ideal women walk
in worship, and the baser sort find sympathy,
and both are bravely stirr'd together as water and oil.

III

But if 'tis ask'd to name what special function it was
that fell sequester'd out of Adam in his lost rib,
and which, when launch'd by Reason on his sea of troubles,
should be his paregoric and comforting cure,—
'twas no unique, ultimatly separable thing,
as is a chemic element; far rather our moods,
influences and spiritual affections are like   930
those many organic substances which, tho' to sense
wholly dissimilar and incomparable in kind,
are yet all combinations of the same simples,
and even in like proportions differently disposed;
so that whether it be starch, oil, sugar, or alcohol
'tis ever our old customers, carbon and hydrogen,
pirouetting with oxygen in their morris antics;
the chemist booketh all of them as C H O,
and his art is as mine, when I but figurate
the twin persistent semitones of my Grand Chant.   940
   And 'twer but bookish, surely, in the fabric of mind
to assume the disposition of vital elements
under a few common names, alike in both sexes;
'tis easier thought that ther is no human faculty
that hath not been in long elaboration of sex
adjusted finely, and often to such richer ends
that, tho' by correlation characters of sex,

(121)

they are not held in subservience to the impulse of Breed,—
as some deem, and impute precocious puberty
to new-born babes, and all their after trouble in life   950
   to shamefast thwarting of inveterat lust.

Now Woman took her jointure from the potency
of spirit stored in flesh, the which, affined to her sex,
became a property of intuition and grew in her,
thru' mutual adaptation with the environments
that wer its own effects, to a female character
in worth alike and weakness distinct from the male:
for while man's Reason drew him whither science led
to walk with downcast eyes fix'd on the ground, and low
incline his ear to catch the sermon-whisper of stones—   960
whence now whole nations, by their treasure-trove enrich'd,
crawl greedily on their knees nosing the soil like swine,
and any, if they can twist their stiffen'd necks about,
see the stars but as stones,—while men thus search'd the earth,
stooping to pick up wisdom, women stood erect
in honest human posture, from light's fount to drink
celestial influences; and this was seen in them
that worship'd Christ nor look'd, as then the apostles did,
for some earthly prosperity or prospect, nor ask'd
what chief seats might be theirs reserved in the Kingdom;   970

his heav'nly call drew him, and the Mary who sat
at Christ's feet in devotion, heard from him her choice
pronounced the one thing needful; and as 'twas for her,
so is it nowaday for us to our happiness.

   For 'tis by such faith only a man can save his soul;
since as his unique spirit cometh more and more
out of slumber into vision, he loseth heart the more
at the inhumanity of nature's omnipotence.
Thatt first savage suspicion is now the last despair
of earnest thinkers, who for love of truth refuse   980
to blink dishonestly the tribulation of man,
but deem it final truth, and see no cure thereof,
nor solace save what brave distraction of thought may bring
in further keen pursuit of knowledge, on the old path
that hath hereby led them where the everlasting worm
eateth their hearts . . . and yet man's Reason (as is confess'd)
since 'tis of nature's fabric must share in her fault;
and man's spiritual sense, which inspireth his grief,
is equally of her giving: whence his complaint sheweth
the strange perversity of creation's self-reproach;   990
tho' nature the while is by beauty awakening
her heav'nly response to her heavenliest desire,
and in spiritual joy sanctioneth to the full
the claim of faith. To such despairers Christ out-spake

in his rich poetry *'Tis better with one eye*
blinded to enter into the life of Goddes Realm
than with both eyes to grieve in Hell. Be thatt not Truth,
then ther is something found for man better than Truth;
which thought wer the supreme vanity of vanities,
at once a superhuman ambition and a poor pride,   1000
truly *the last infirmity of* his *noble mind.*

From blind animal passion to the vision of Spirit
all actual gradations come of natur, and each
severally in time and place is answerable in man.
As with the embryo which in normal growth passeth
thru' evolutionary stages, at each stage
consisting with itself agreeably, so Mind
may be by observation in young changes waylaid,
agreeable all, tho' no more congruous with themselves
than what a baby thinketh of its naked feet,   1010
when first it is aware of them, is like the thought
of piteous sympathy with which when an old man
he wil come to regard them. So likewise of BREED,
youth and age hold their irreconcilable extremes,
from him who deemeth sex to be the curse of man
to him who findeth in it the only pleasur of life:

III

then the four temperaments of blood possess of kind
their different sensibilities, and every bias
of education coloureth; while in abstract thought
some would submit its energy to rule of state,   1020
to ethic duty some, others to personal health,
to social propriety or the grace of good manners;
climate can subjugate and religion constrain;
national taste prescribe practice and fix ideals;
yet howso no two men wil be found wholly alike,
nor any one man always consonant in himself;
the saint wil hav his days of humiliation and trial,
the clown his rare moments of revelation and peace,
while commonsense wil waver in its faith with fortune.

Now as a physical object apparent to sense   1030
must in all its perspectivs be studied, tho' none
be true wholly in itself, and reality is found
by elimination of error, so 'twil be with Love,
which, if it had no various aspects of feeling
nor delusiv perspectivs to spiritual sight,
neither coud it hav any essential property
in the Wisdom of God: thus men, who mostly liv
in the light of one aspect and convinced thereby,
wil deem of love differently, and in as many ways
as ther be planes of spirit and faculties of mind: 1040

and the philosopher expecteth little audience
of men school'd to the habit of their own liking,
and wer he heaven-inspired he should not therefor look
to win the general ear; yet, one proviso allow'd,
he may command agreement; so (saith he) if ther be
any one scheme of Reason in the evolution of Mind
preferable and probable—and without so much faith
he would sit dumb—then thatt ideal wil be found
in few, not in many, but potential in them,
and in the best imperfect, a desire of all,   1050
an everlasting hope not everlastingly
to be rebuff'd and baffled, rather prëordain'd
by arch-creativ Wisdom, as man groweth to find
his Will in Goddes pleasur, his pleasur in Goddes Will;
drawn to thatt happiness by the irresistible
predominant attraction, which worketh secure
in mankind's Love of Beauty and in the Beauty of Truth.

Art is the true and happy science of the soul,
exploring nature for spiritual influences,
as doth physical science for comforting powers,   1060
advancing so to a sure knowledge with like progress:
but lovers who thereto look for expression of truth

III

hav great need to remember that no plastic Art,
tho' it create ideals noble as are the forms
that Pheidias wrought, can ever elude or wholly escape
its earthly medium; nor in its adumbrations
reach thatt detach'd suprasensuous vision, whereto
Poetry and Music soar, nor dive down in the mine
where cold philosophy diggeth her fiery jewels—
or only by rare magic may it sometimes escape.   1070

   And this was the intuition of our landscape-painters,
whose venture seem'd humbled in renouncing the prize
of the classic contest, when like truants from school
they made off to the fields with their satchels, and came
on nature's beauteous by-paths into a purer air:
For the Art of painting, by triumph of colouring
enticed to Realism, had confounded thereby
its own higher intention, and in portrayal of spirit
made way for Symbolism which, tho' it stand aloof,
is outfaced in the presence of direct feeling: 1080
Sithence in presentation of feminin beauty
the highest Art lost mastery of its old ideal;
as in the great pictur of the two Women at a Well,
where Titian's young genius, devising a new thing,
employ'd the plastic power to exhibit at once
two diverse essences in their value and contrast;

(127)

for while by the æsthetic idealisation of form
his earthly love approacheth to celestial grace,
his draped Uranian figure is by symbols veil'd,
and in pictorial Beauty suffereth defeat: 1090
Yea, despite all her impregnable confidence
in the truth of her wisdom, as there she sitteth
beside the fountain, dazzlingly apparel'd, enthroned,
with thoughtful face impassiv, averting her head
as 'twer for fuller attention so to incline an ear
to the impartial hearing of the importunat plea
of the other, who over-against her on the cornice-plinth
posturing her wonted nakedness in sensuous ease,
leaneth her body to'ards her, and with imploring grace
urgeth the vain deprecation of her mortal prayer.   1100

   Giorgione, his master, already had gone to death
plague-stricken at prime, when Titian painted thatt picture,
donning his rival's mantle, and strode to higher fame—
yet not by this canvas; he who had it, hid it;
nor won it public favour when it came to light,
untill some mystic named it in the Italian tongue
L'Amor Sacro e Profano, and so rightly divined;
for tho' ther is no record save the work of the brush
to tell the intention, yet what the mind wrought is there;

and who looketh thereon may see in the two left arms 1110
the symbolism apportioning the main design;
for while the naked figure with extended arm
and outspredd palm vauntingly balanceth aloft
a little lamp, whose flame lost in the bright daylight
wasteth in the air, thatt other hath the arm bent down
and oppositely nerved, and clencheth with gloved hand
closely the cover'd vessel of her secret fire.

Thus Titian hath pictured the main sense of my text,
and this truth: that as Beauty is all with Spirit twined,
so all obscenity is akin to the ugliness 1120
which Art would outlaw; whence cometh thatt tinsel honour
and mimicry of beauty which is the attire of vice.

Allegory is a cloudland inviting fancy
to lend significance to chancey shapes; and here
I deem not that the child, who playeth between the Loves
at Titian's well, was pictured by him with purpose
to show the first contact of love with boyhood's mind;
and yet never was symbol more deftly devised:
Mark how the child looking down on the water see'th
only a reflection of the realities—as 'twas 1130
with the mortals in Plato's cave—nor more of them

than Moses saw of God; he can see but their backs,
save for a shifty glimpse of the pleading profil
of earthly Love (which also is subtle truth); and most
how in his play his plunged hand stirreth to and fro
both images together in a confused dazzle
of the dancing ripples as he gazeth intent.

THE TESTAMENT

OF BEAUTY

BOOK IV

Ethick

BEAUTY, the eternal Spouse of the Wisdom of God
and Angel of his Presence thru' all creation,
fashioning her new love-realm in the mind of man,
attempteth every mortal child with influences
of her divine supremacy . . . ev'n as in a plant
when the sap mounteth secretly and its wintry stalk
breaketh out in the prolific miracle of Spring,
or as the red blood floodeth into a beating heart
to build the animal body comely and strong; so she
in her transcendant rivalry would flush his spirit   10

with pleasurable ichor of heaven: and where she hath found
responsiv faculty in some richly favour'd soul—
L'anima vaga delle cose belle, as saith
the Florentine,—she wil inaugurate her feast
of dedication, and even in thatt earliest onset,
when yet infant Desire hath neither goal nor clue
to fix the dream, ev'n then, altho' it graspeth nought
and passeth in its airy vision away, and dieth
out of remembrance, 'tis in its earnest of life
and dawn of bliss purer and hath less of earthly tinge   20
than any other after-attainment of the understanding:
for all man's knowledge kenneth also of toil and flaw,
and even his noblest works, tho' they illume the dark
with individual consummation, are cast upon
by the irrelevant black shadows of time and fate.

Hence is the fascination of amateurs in art,
who renouncing accomplishment attain the prize
of their humbler devotion,—as Augustin saith,
that fools may come at holiness where wise men miss,
Facit enim hoc quaedam etiam stoliditas,—   30
arriving by short-coming, like to homely birds
of passage, nesting on the roofs of the workshops.
And tho' of secret knowledge man's art is compáct,
yet not the loving study of any master-work,

nor longest familiarity can ever efface
its birthday of surprisal; and great music to me
is glorify'd by memory of one timeless hour
when all thought fled scared from me in my bewilderment.

  See then the boy in first encounter with beauty,
his nativ wonder awaken'd by the motion of love;   40
as when live air, breathing upon a smother'd fire,
shooteth the smouldering core with tiny flames—so he
kindleth at heart with eternal expectancies,
and the dream within him looketh out at his eyes.

  'Twas thru' worship of Christ that this thing came to men,
whereat, when art achieved portrayal of tenderness,
the christian painters throng'd their heav'n with cherubims,
little amorini, who with rebel innocence
dispossess'd the tall angels; and Mary's young babe
cast-off his swaddling bands, and stood-up on her lap   50
in grace of naked childhood for the image of God.

  But as 'tis with the Race, for which our hope draweth
the only assurance of its high nobility
from rare examples, holy men and wise, revered
ev'n by the common folk, that none the less pursue
their common folly interminably, and more and more
pamper despair that is the giant sorrow of earth—
so in the child this glimpse or touch of immanence,

being a superlativ brief moment of glory,

is too little to leaven the inveterate lump of life;   60

and the instincts whose transform'd vitality should lust

after spiritual things, return to their vomit

and wallow in the mire of their animal ruts.

    Nature hath something truly of her promise in all:

yet, in the infinit disposition of random seeds,

her full potency is rare; as in the end of his book

that maketh the old school-benches yet to sprout in green,

Aristotle confesseth: where the teacher saith

virtue cannot be taught to a mind not well disposed

by natur, and he that hath thatt rarest excelence,   70

διά τινας θείας αἰτίας, may be above all men   .

styled truly fortunat; and with those four Greek words

hath proudly prick'd to virtue many a sluggard soul.

    Forsooth the need of Fortune stayeth not here, alas!

Ther is no assurance of stability or fair growth,

unless she stand by faithfully and foster the soul,

fending from all evil and encompassing with good,

the while these intimations come to be understood

and harmonized by Reason in the conduct of life.

    Now as Reason matured to the power of manhood,   8c .

tutor'd by disciplin of natur, and ordering

the accumulated scrutiny of physical flux

in various sciences, so education of spirit,
.in the dignity of its creativ enthusiasms
and honorable intelligence of Goddes gifts,
mapp'd out its own science of conduct, aligning
a pathway of happiness thru' the valley of death:
and thatt science, call'd Ethick, dealing with the skill
and manage of the charioteer in Plato's myth,
rangeth up here in place for the parley of this book.   90

Since all Ethick implyeth a sense of Duty in man,
'tis first to enquire whence that responsible OUGHT arose;
a call so universal and plain-spoken that some
hav abstracted a special faculty, distinct
from animal bias and underivable,
whereby the creature kenneth the creator's Will,
that, in stillness of sound speaking to gentle souls,
dowereth all silence with the joy of his presence;
but to men savage or superstitious a voice
of horror, maleficent, inescapable,   100
hounding them with fearful conviction of sin, as when
Adam in Eden hid from the scour of God's eye.
Which old tale of displeasur is true to life: because
the imperativ obligation cannot be over-summ'd,

being in itself the self-conscience of thatt Essence
which is no other indeed than the prime ordinance
that we call Law of Nature,—in its grade the same
with the determin'd habit of electrons, the same
with the determining instinct of unreasoning life,
NECESSITY become conscient in man—whereto   110
all insubordination is imperfection in kind.

    Reality appeareth in forms to man's thought
as several links interdependent of a chain
that circling returneth upon itself, as doth
the coil'd snake that in art figureth eternity.
    From Universal Mind the first-born atoms draw
their function, whose rich chemistry the plants transmute
to make organic life, whereon animals feed
to fashion sight and sense and give service to man,
who sprung from them is conscient in his last degree   120
of ministry unto God, the Universal Mind,
whither all effect returneth whence it first began.
    The Ring in its repose is Unity and Being:
Causation and Existence are the motion thereof.
Thru'out all runneth Duty, and the conscience of it
is thatt creativ faculty of animal mind
that, wakening to self-conscience of all Essences,

closeth the full circle, where the spirit of man
escaping from the bondage of physical Law
re-entereth eternity by the vision of God.   130

This absolution of Reason is not for all to see:
But any man may picture how Duty was born,
and trace thereafter its passage in the ethick of man.
    Ther is a young black ouzel, now building her nest
under the Rosemary on the wall, suspiciously
shunning my observation as I sit in the porch,
intentiv with my pencil as she with her beak: ·
Coud we discourse together, and wer I to ask for-why
she is making such pother with thatt rubbishy straw,
her answer would be surely: 'I know not, but I MUST.'   140
Then coud she take persuasion of Reason to desist
from a purposeless action, in but a few days hence
when her eggs wer to hatch, she would look for her nest;
and if another springtide found us here again,
with memory of her fault, she would know a new word,
having made conscient passage from the MUST to the OUGHT.
    I halt not then nor stumble at how the duteous call
was gotten in course of nature, rather it lieth to show
how it was after-shapen in man from physical
to moral ends, and came no longer only to affirm   150

but sometimes even to oppose the bidding of instinct,
positing beside OUGHT the equivalent OUGHT NOTS,
the stern forbiddances of those tables of stone
that Moses fetch'd out of the thunder of Sinai.

And since we see how man's judgment of Right and Wrong
varieth with education—and thatt without effect
to strengthen or weaken Duty—, we conclude therefrom
that education shapeneth our moralities.
And when and whereas Conscience transfigureth the Instincts
—to affection, as aforesaid, from motherly selfhood,   160
and to spiritual love from lust of breed—, we find
Duty therewith extended in the moral field.
Thus 'tis (as missionaries tell) that head-hunters
who seek relish in refinement of cruelty,
wil yet to soft feelings respond at gentle appeal:
my dog would do as well, coud he understand my speech.
Yet tho' we see how birds in catering for their young
stint not their self-devotion, and punctiliously observe
distributiv justice; and that dutiful dogs
urged by conflicting calls wil stand awhile perplex'd   170
in dumb deliberation—ne'ertheless, because
the true spiritual combat is unknown to brutes,
moralists teaching virtue as an end-in-itself
repudiate any sanction from motivs engaged

on animal welfare, and make utility
a cant term of reproach; tho' on their higher plane
spiritual conduct also is utilitarian:
For virtue subserveth the soul's comfort and joy,
therewithal no less useful, nay more requisit
than is material comfort to our full happiness   180
in self-realization of perfected nature;
the which a sound doctrin of pleasure wil confirm.

   Denial of Use hath done our virtue wrong, while some
belittle also our Ethick, saying the subject is
of matter unknowledgeable in scientific sense,
taking contingency from the imperfection of man.
Granted, wer all men perfect, none would seek virtue;
nor should I now debate of it; but neither again
wer all omniscient, would any seek knowledge:
yet go we hunting after truth insatiably   190
as the Saints after holiness, who, comforted
by least attainment, persevere,—*Seeking the Lord
whom they hav found*: and if a check or fault show more
in Ethick, 'tis that the hunter is on fuller cry
after true happiness than after mental truth;
or he thinketh at least to hav well nosed his desire,
and he nameth his quarry 'Satisfaction of soul.'
Whereas of absolute Truth, whatever thatt may be,

or is, he hath not an inkling, nay nor any cause,
save in spiritual faith, ev'n to hope well of it.
('Tis for such lack of stand that deep thinkers, who plot
intellectual approaches to the unknown, wil lean
unconsciously upon ethick, or in the end incline
graciously to'ards it.) Now any deficiency
is more discernible in an object known than in
a thing unknown to us, and in the discussion of it
    ther is better likelihood of agreement.

Altho' good disposition (as Aristotle hath it)
may be by beauty educated, and aspire
to theoretic wisdom (as Plato would teach)   210
and Ethick therewithal claim honor of the same rank
that ideal philosophy ascribeth to man,
yet, if for lack of faith he sink that claim, I see
a thing of hap without place in Reality.
    On no hand is't deny'd that terms of Right and Wrong
are wholly pertinent to man's condition on earth;
nor that, whatever his destiny may be, his origin
was bestial and his first ethick a rudiment,
that shifting ever and shaping in the story of man
at every time is the index of his growth in grace;   220
and, if the change of customs that the herd adopt

for comfort and to insure what they most value in life,
hath moral tendency upward, then thatt tendency is
the animal sanction of virtue, and wil take honor as such.

But Duty instill'd with order is so almighty of kind
that 'twil make Law of Habit, whence all social codes
outlast their turn and time, and in arrear of life
hold the common folk backward from their nobler vaunt,
lagging and dragging, whether as a garment outgrown
tatter'd and foolish, or as strong fetters and chains   230
wherein *they lie fast-bound in misery and iron.*

Hence cometh all the need and fame of TEACHERS, men
of inborn nobility, call'd Prophets of God,
Saviours of society, Seers of the promised land,—
thatt white-filleted company that Aeneas found
circled around Musæus in the Elysian fields,
the loved and loveable whose names liv evermore,
the sainted pioneers of salvation, unto whom
all wisdom won and all man's future hope is due;
and with inspiration of their ampler air we see   240
cur Ethick split up shear and sharply atwain; two kinds
diverse in kind ther be; the one of social need,
lower, stil holding backward in the clutch of earth,
from old animal bondage unredeem'd; the other
higher and spiritual, that by personal affiance

with beauty hath made escape, soaring away to where
the Ring of Being closeth in the Vision of God.

Sticklers for equality wil hear nought of this,
arguing that social is but a past-personal,
personal a future-social, tenses of one verb,   250
the *amatum* and *amabo* on the stem of 'love,'
virtue's pure nativ stock which hath no need of graft;
—a doctrin kindly at heart, that cajoleth alike
diffidence of the ruler and conceit of the crowd,
who in collusion float its credit; and awhile
their ship of state runneth like the yacht in the race
that with full bellying sail, for lack of seamanship,
seemeth to forge ahead while it loseth leeway.

No Politick admitteth nor did ever admit
the teacher into confidence: nay ev'n the Church,   260
with hierarchy in conclave compassing to install
Saint Peter in Cæsar's chair, and thereby win for man
the promises for which they had loved and worship'd Christ,
relax'd his heav'nly code to stretch her temporal rule.
For social Ethick with its legalized virtue
is but in true semblance, àlike for praise or blame,
a friendly domestication of man's old wolf-foe,
the adaptable subservient gentlemanly dog,
beneath groom'd coat and collar in his passion unchanged.

IV

Thus 'tis that levelers, deeming all ethick one,   270
and for being Socialists thinking themselves Teachers,
can preach class-hatred as the enlighten'd gospel of love;
but should they look to find firm scientific ground,
whereon to found their creed in the true history
of social virtue and of its progress hitherto,
'twil be with them in their research, as 'twas with him
who yesteryear sat down in Mesopotamy
to dig out Abram's birthplace in the lorn grave-yard
of Asian monarchies;—and low hummocks of dust
betray where legendary cities lie entomb'd,   280
Chaldæan KISH and UR; while for all life today
poor nomads, with their sparse flotilla of swarthy tents
and slow sand-faring camels, cruise listlessly o'erhead,
warreners of the waste: Now this man duly unearth'd
the walls whence Terah flitted, but beneath those walls
more walls, and the elder buildings of a dynasty
of wider rule than Abram knew, a nation extinct
ere he was born: where-thru' sinking deeper their shafts
the diggers came yet never on virgin soil, but stil
wondering on earlier walls, arches and masonry,   290
a city and folk undremt of in archæology,
trodden-under ere any story of man began; and there,
happening on the king's tomb, they shovel'd from the dust

the relics of thatt old monarch's magnificence—
Drinking vessels of beaten silver or of clean gold,
vases of alabaster, obsidian chalices,
cylinder seals of empire and delicat gems
of personal adornment, ear-rings and finger-rings,
craftsmen's tools copper and golden, and for music a harp;
withal in silver miniatur his six-oar'd skiff,   300
a model in build and trim of such as ply today
Euphrates' flowery marshes: all his earthly toys
gather'd to him in his grave, that he might nothing lack
in the unknown life beyond, but find ready to hand
his jewel'd dice and gaming board and chamber-lamp,
his toilet-box of paints and unguents—Therefore 'twas
the chariot of his pride whereon he still would ride
was buried with him; there lay yet the enamel'd film
of the inlaid perish'd wood, and all the metal gauds
that had emboss'd the rail: animal masks in gold,   310
wild bulls and lions, and twin-figured on the prow
great panther-heads to glare in silver o'er the course,
impatient of their spring: and one rare master-work
whose grace the old warrior wist not should outliv the name
and fame of all his mighty doings, when he set it up
thatt little nativ donkey, his mascot on the pole.

   'Twas he who dug told me of these things and how,

finding himself a housebreaker in the home of men
who sixty hundred years afore, when they left life,
had seal'd their tombs from sacrilege and there had lain,   320
til from the secresy of their everlasting sleep
he had torn the coverlet—his spirit, dazed awhile
in wonder, suddenly was strick'n with great horror;
for either side the pole, where lay the harness'd bones
of the yoke-mated oxen, there beside their bones
lay the bones of the grooms, and slaughter'd at their post
all the king's body-guard, each liegeman spear in hand,
in sepulchred attention; and whereby lay the harp
the arm-bones of the player, as there she had pluck'd her dirge,
lay mingled with its fragments; and nearby disposed,   330
two rows of skeletons, her sisterly audience
whose lavish ear-pendants and gold-filleted hair,
the uniform decoration of their young service,
mark'd them for women of the harem, sacrificed
to accompany their lord, the day when he set forth
to enter into the presence of the scepter'd shades
congregated with splendour in the mansions of death.

    Leave Tigris now and Ur. Seek out our Aryan race
by Gunga and Hydaspes in the teeming realm
where Sakya Muni preach'd of gentleness and love,   340
and took divinity before Christ came: see how

at every Rajah's pyre, in Punjab or Kashmire,

in Vijayanóggar, Kalikata and Udaipur,

for liv-long centuries the mild Hindus hav burnt

their multitudinous girl-concubines alive,

and still beneath our lax imperial rule wil deem

any honest outlawry of their ritual Suttee

a tyrannous impiety of our western manners;

which none the less withheld not of our island kings

the last Henry, styled first Defendër of the Faith,   350

from slaying his wives at will; nor was he for such crime

less esteem'd of the folk; altho' judged as a man

by pagan ethick or christian or by the insight

of poet or historian, more despicable

than we need to suppose thatt old monarch of Ur.

   See how cross-eyed the pride of our world-wide crusade

against Nigerian slavery, while the London poor

in their Victorian slums lodged closer and filthier

than the outraged alien; and under liberty's name

our Industry is worse fed and shut out from the sun.—   360

In every age and nation a like confusion is found.

————•————

IF DUTY held us long, now as in the old adage

IV

PLEASURE may follow after, taking like second rank
in Plato's myth, as I twist it: wherein we traced
Duty from the selfhood of individual life
growing to reach communion with life eternal;
while in the younger horse was pleasur intensified
by love, untill it issueth in the love of God.
And yet hath pleasure truly its main stronghold in Self,
because the greatest pleasure that man knoweth, is aye   370
the pleasur of life, even as his chief displeasur is death.

   This Life-joy, like the breath-kiss of the all-ambient air
unnoticed til the lack of it bring pain and death,
is coefficient with the untrammel'd energy
of nativ faculty, and the autometric scale
of all functions and motions, which in the animal
struggle for Self persistently against all hindrance:
it is the lordly heraldry of the banner'd flower,
in brutes the vaunt of vigour and the pose of pride,
their wild impersonation of majesty; and in man   380
the grace and ease of health alike in body and mind,
thatt right congruity of his parts, for lack whereof
his sanity is disabled maim'd and compromised.
From personal pleasure then, seeing how good it is,
and how a good man's pleasures all are good, it came
an easy thought for men in quest of happiness

to take it for their aim in all conduct, the account
and logic of Ethick. So, flaunting their motto
"Pleasure for pleasure's sake," these doughty Hedonists,
having got rid of whatsoever oldfashion'd king   390
had ruled by right divine, chose out for his good looks
and crown'd this gay pretender, against whose privilege
men in the street and schoolmen are for once agreed;
because none wil deny that some pleasures are bad,
while all men honour them who for their honour's sake
wil suffer pain, and risk the great displeasur of death.

  Pure Hedonism therefore is confuted off-hand;
and its social pretension is but a will-o-the-wisp;
as if the honest pleasur of a wise man coud lie
in furthering or conniving-at the pleasur of them   400
who know not ev'n their own unhappiness, nor how
ere they can win happiness they must learn wisdom
by paths difficult and to them unpleasurable.
Nor is spiritual Hedonism in better plight,
for some are found to take spiritual pleasur in crime.

  'Twould seem then the prime task of Ethick to discern
'twixt pleasures good and bad: but first 'twer well to show
how ever it came that Pleasure, being the champïon
of our integrity, should in the event appear
virtue's insidious foe; for-sure ther is no knowledge   410

in the wisdom of conduct cardinal as is this.

  Now in my thought the manner of it was on this wise—
As Pleasure came in man to the conscience of self,
his Reason abstracted it as an idea, and when
he found the pleasur increasing with the conscience of it,
he dwelt thereon, and seeking more and more to enrich
his conscious pleasur, and bloating it with luxury,
invented and indulged vices unknown to brutes.
Thus was nature's intention thwarted: whereupon
(seeing also how brooding upon sensual delight   420
provoketh the desire, which, so long as the mind
be but engaged healthily or distracted apart,
would never rise to emotion) Moralists took fright,
and Teachers banishing pleasure from Ethick, where
they should hav been content with a danger-signal,
posted a prohibition, and not only forbade
pleasur as a motiv for any conduct, but ruled
that any admixtur of intention or its chance presence
deprived conduct of merit: whence pleasure with them,
instead of being an in-itself absolute good   430
as nature would have had it, and which man would wish
to be always present and with his perfection increase,
came to be bann'd as the pollution of virtue;—And so,
when the young poet my companion in study

and friend of my heart refused a peach at my hands,
he being then a housecarl in Loyola's menie,
'twas that he fear'd the savor of it, and when he waived
his scruple to my banter, 'twas to avoid offence.
But I, upon thatt day which after fifty years
is near as yesterday, was no stranger to fear   440
of pleasure, but had grown fearful of thatt fear; yet since
the sublimation of life whereto the Saints aspire
is a self-holocaust, their sheer asceticism
is justified in them; the more because the bent
and nativ color of mind that leadeth them aloof,
or driveth, is thatt very delicacy of sense,
whereby a pinprick or a momentary whiff
or hairbreadth motion freëth the detent of force
that can distract them wholly from their high pursuit:
wherefor they fly God's garden, whose forbidden fruit   450
(seemeth to them) was sweeten'd by a fiend's desire
to make them fond and foolish. Nature ne'ertheless
singeth loud in her prison, and for all ecstasy
these mystics find no language but to echo again
the psalm of her captivity; nay, furthermore,
the doctrin esoteric in their rapt divines
and their diviner poets—this the novice knew—
is the rëincarnation of their renounced desire.

Repudiation of pleasur is a reason'd folly
of imperfection. Ther is no motiv can rebate   460
or decompose the intrinsic joy of activ life,
whereon all function whatsoever in man is based.
Consider how this mortal sensibility
hath a wide jurisdiction of range in all degrees,
from mountainous gravity to imperceptible
faintest tenuities:—The imponderable fragrance
of my window-jasmin, that from her starry cup
of red-stemm'd ivory invadeth my being,
as she floateth it forth, and wantoning unabash'd
asserteth her idea in the omnipotent blaze   470
of the tormented sun-ball, checquering the grey wall
with shadow-tracery of her shapely fronds; this frail
unique spice of perfumery, in which she holdeth
monopoly by royal licence of Nature,
is but one of a thousand angelic species,
original beauties that win conscience in man:
a like marvel hangeth o'er the rosebed, and where
the honeysuckle escapeth in serpentine sprays
from its dark-cloister'd clamber thru' the old holly-bush,
spreading its joybunches to finger at the sky   480
in revel above rivalry. Legion is their name;
Lily-of-the-vale, Violet, Verbena, Mignonette,

Hyacinth, Heliotrope, Sweet-briar, Pinks and Peas,
Lilac and Wallflower, or such white and purple blooms
that sleep i' the sun, and their heavy perfumes withhold
to mingle their heart's incense with the wonder-dreams,
love-laden prayers and reveries that steal forth from earth,
under the dome of night: and tho' these blossomy breaths,
that hav presumed the title of their gay genitors,
enter but singly into our neighboring sense, that hath   490
no panorama, yet the mind's eye is not blind
unto their multitudinous presences:—I know
that if odour wer visible as color is, I'd see
the summer garden aureoled in rainbow clouds,
with such warfare of hues as a painter might choose
to show his sunset sky or a forest aflame;
while o'er the country-side the wide clover-pastures
and the beanfields of June would wear a mantle, thick
as when in late October, at the drooping of day
the dark grey mist arising blotteth out the land   500
with ghostly shroud. Now these and such-like influences
of tender specialty must not—so fine they be—
fall in neglect and all their loveliness be lost,
being to the soul deep springs of happiness, and full
of lovingkindness to the natural man, who is apt
kindly to judge of good by comfortable effect.

IV

Thus all men ever hav judged the wholesomness of food
from the comfort of body ensuing thereupon,
whereby all animals retrieve their proper diet;
but if when in discomfort 'tis for pleasant hope   510
of health restored we swallow nauseous medicines,
so mystics use asceticism, yea, and no man
readier than they to assert eventual happiness
to justify their conduct. Whence it is not strange
(for so scientific minds in search of truth digest
assimilable hypotheses) they should extend
their pragmatism, and from their happiness deduce
the very existence and the natur of God, and take
religious consolation for the ground of faith:
as if the pleasur of life wer the sign-manual   520
of Nature when she set her hand to her covenant.

But man, vain of his Reason and thinking more to assure
its independence, wil disclaim complicity
with human emotion; and regarding his Mother
deemeth it dutiful and nobler in honesty
coldly to criticize than purblindly to love;
and in pride of this quarrel he hath been led in the end
to make distinction of kind 'twixt Pleasur and Happiness;
observing truly enough how one may hav pleasure
and yet miss happiness; but this warpeth the sense   530

and common use of speech, since all tongues in the world
call children and silly folk happy and sometimes ev'n brutes.

 The name of happiness is but a wider term
for the unalloy'd conditions of the Pleasur of Life,
attendant on all function, and not to be deny'd
to th' soul, unless forsooth in our thought of nature
spiritual is by definition unnatural.

 But I would not thus wrong nature; rather say I
that as man realizeth his higher energies,
the quality and value of his pleasures wil so change,   540
that tho' the animal life-joy persist thru'out,
yet his transported joy developing thereon
cometh by excelence to need a special term.
And Aristotle in his tenth book thus summeth it—
"Whatso thatt faculty may be which hath in man
"natural governance and apprehendeth things
"noble and divine,—it is the energy (so saith he)
"of thatt faculty in its proper excelence, which is
"the Perfect Happiness;" and with his predicate
he assumeth the less perfect also, and lower states.   550
But these philosophers—their Ethick being concern'd
with man's perfection—used the abstracted terms whereby
they had pre-defined distinctions, which as they diverged
in separat culmination obscured identity.

'Twas for that reason, I guess, that Aristotle himself
so harpeth on his doctrin, as if he was aware
that his conclusion had somehow miss'd its full premiss:
But if we see Spiritual, Mental and Animal
to be gradations merged together in growth and mix'd
in their gradations, and that the animal pleasure   560
runneth thru'out all grades heartening all energies,
then Aristotle's wisdom goeth without saying;
and the actüal complexity of human conduct
wil appear nature's order in the condition of growth;
and so the trouble and wonderment of baulk'd insight
may ali be presently sponged from the treatises.

   Altho' in the distinction of pleasures good and bad
the unparagon'd nobility of the great virtues
standeth without controversy among them that know
—who instill them as duties—, yet they hav writ no rule   570
nor rubric whereby conduct can in lesser affairs
accommodate these principles, when they conflict
in upright personalities, nor square their use
with the intricat contingencies that knit our lives,
and the interaction of unrelated sequences.
In thatt uncharted jungle a good man wil go right,
while an ill disposition wil miss and go wrong:
yet in the worst we stil may find something to praise,

in the lame child that stumbleth, or the canker'd bud;
ev'n the poor blasted promise of desiderat fruit   580
hath true relation to the absent beauty thereof.

Forever on the asses bridge and in the ship of fools
life is agog; and there the Muse hath set her stage,
and in humorous compact with philosophy
hideth her godlike face beneath a grinning mask,
and donning the gay motley of idiotic man
empersonateth him in his chance dilemmas;
by the eternal comedy of the unfitness of things
beguiling the disconsolat with sympathy
and cheering contemplation with æsthetic mirth.   590
Full many hav found happiness toiling all their time
thus disporting with truth; and at carving such toys
hav thru' love of children become Teachers of men:
But here *I wol nat han to do of swich matere.*

Since then all promise of spiritual advancement
lieth in two things, good disposition and (as 'twas said)
right education, it followeth here to speak of these.

First then of Disposition.—Unless ther truly be
more good than bad absolutely in the make of man,
ther is no security for him and little hope,   600
except the inherent harmony and unity of good

be such as must in the end outweigh the surplusage
of all discordant enmity; and this well may be:
but should we inquire if Nature hath by any means
inclined man's disposition to the virtuous choice,
we may find how she hath done this, and by the energy
of the imitativ faculty hath assured her end.
"For Mimicry is inborn in man from childhood up:
"and in this differeth he from other animals,
"being the most imitativ: and his first approach   610
"to learning maketh he in mimicry, and hath delight
"in imitations of all kinds." I would indeed
that Aristotle had set this pregnant verity
in forefront of his Ethick also, as now 'tis found
to stablish his Poetick; for the assumption of it
here and there in the Morals escapeth notice
and all the consequences thereof are unseen.
But if the cradled child imitateth the shows
that happen around him, he for-sure wil most attend
to those that most attract, and must therefore be drawn   620
and held by the inborn love of Beauty inconsciently
of preference to imitate the more beautiful things.
And because Virtue is an activity, and lieth not
in doctrin and theory but in practice and conduct,
co-ordinating potencies into energy,

(and here 'tis Aristotle again speaketh, not I)
the preferential imitation of right action
is THE HABIT OF VIRTUE: and thus a child well-bred
in good environment, so soon as he is aware
of personality, wil know and think himself   630
a virtuous being and instinctivly, in the proud
realization of Self common to all animals,
becometh to be his own ideal, a such-a-one
as would WILL and DO this (saith he) and never do thatt,
refraining there from shame, consenting here for love,
winning new beauty of soul from the embrace of beauty,
and strength by practised combat against folly and wrong,
to perfect as he may his idea of himself.

Spiritual life being thus imagin'd in the child
thru' conscient personality and love of beauty,   640
—which on so tender a plant budding hath power to bear
the richest fruit of all creation, incomparable—
ther is nought in all his nurtur of more intrinsic need
than is the food of Beauty: as mammal's milk to his flesh,
which admitteth no proxy, so Beauty is to his soul,
that calleth for this comforting of nature's breast,
tho' its outcries be unheard when it pineth in pain:
and since the hunger of mimicry is so strong in him,
that in the lack of milk 'twil ravin gall, and draw

infection and death from evil as quickly as life from good,
the first intrinsic need in education is found. 651

Thus Christ, who knew what was in man and taught
man's perfect happiness to be the wonted realm
of heav'n within his heart, spake thus 𝕮𝖆𝖐𝖊 𝖍𝖊𝖉𝖊 (he said)
𝕾𝖊 𝖙𝖍𝖆𝖙 𝖞𝖊 𝖔𝖋𝖋𝖊𝖓𝖉𝖊 𝖓𝖔𝖙 𝖜𝖔𝖓 𝖔𝖋 𝖙𝖍𝖊𝖘𝖊 𝖑𝖎𝖙𝖊𝖑𝖑 𝖜𝖔𝖓𝖘:
and once again on this wise, "If ther be any sin
"unpardonable even in the wide compassion of God,
"'tis the denial and blasphemy of his Holy Spirit,
"and the quenching in others of its nascent flame."

Delicat and subtle are the dealings of nature, 660
whereby the emotionable sense secretly is touch'd
to awareness and by glimpse of heav'nly vision drawn
within the attraction of the creativ energy
that is the ultimat life of all being soe'er:
While Science sitteth apart in her exile, attent
on her other own invisibles; and working back
to the atoms, she handleth their action to harness
the gigantic forces of eternal motion,
in serviceable obedience to man's mortal needs;
and not to be interrupted nor call'd off her task, 670
dreaming, amid the wonders of her sightly works,
thru' her infinitesimals to arrive at last
at the unsearchable immensities of Goddes realm.

But while the intellectual faculty is yet unborn,
spiritual things to children are even as Music is,
thatt firstborn pleasur of animal conscience that now
hath for its human honour its origin forgot;
the which a child absorbeth readily and without thought,
tho' in after years, if thatt initiation hav lack'd,
scarce can a man by grammar come at the elements.   680
Their twain affinity may be seen also in this,
that both are companied by the same full delight
of progress in performance, while the same method
serveth for both; if but the teacher be himself
virtuous or musical—an examplar as such,
he wil be keenly follow'd, and often in his love
that his pupil surpass him is his best reward.

Of intellectual training 'tis not here to tell;
thatt cometh later, and then the trouble is evermore
the lack of teachers; yet wer teachers plentiful,   690
and gentle environment as common as bramble-scrub,
never coud human wit discern to accommodate
the countless idiosyncracies of mind withal;
indeterminable are they and never can be told.
But 'twer well to consider in what a fusty crypt
the awakening mind is caged when—like a butterfly

that newly hath slipp'd its crysalis to sport i' the sun—
it thrusteth out its finely adapted tentacles
in their first palping movements to the encounter of life,
with confidence exploring its nativ yearnings.   700
How, when this apprehensiv expectancy is met
by fenced obstruction! How, when ev'n the syllables
which with such duteous pains the child had learn'd to tongue,
the secret spell whereat the fabled treasure-house
should open its doors—how, when thatt magic Sesamë
hath proved a foreign jargon and, like a rusty key,
by long mishandling already hath hamper'd the lock!
How should not childish effort, thus thwarted and teased,
recoil dishearten'd bruized and stupefy'd beneath
the rough-shod inculcation of inculcated minds,   710
case-harden'd by their own thoughtless reiterations?

    The mud-fish may be happy and at home in the pond,
but live Imagination, conscient of its joy,
ranketh oft with the dunces in such scholarship,
finding its happiness in freedom to mature
the personality of its nativ potency.
Others in after-growth at heavy cost repair
their early damage, since in intellectual things
all errors are remediable; but 'tis not so
in the spiritual life, nay ev'n the soul wash'd pure   720

of absorb'd taint may take a strange gloss of the lye.

Of two young thoro'breds galoping neck to neck
I'd choose the colt that with least effort held his course.
Of two runners abreast my liking would crown him
who had greater grace of limb and show'd no trouble of face,
tho' he by such complacency might miss the prize:
But virtue in the soldier is the martyr's heart
that, battling for supremacy, out-stayeth defeat,
firing the citadel ere he yield it to the foe:
and 'tis nobility that pulleth our favour   730
upon the weaker side in any unequal match.
   Now in spiritual combat, altho' I must deem
them the most virtuous who with least effort excell,
yet, virtue being a conflict, moralisers hold
that where conflict is hardest virtue must be at best;
and in the rub of life and physical hindrance
a man who has striven heroically and done great deeds,
in spite of frailty or bodily disease or pain,
may win more admiration and praise in the end than he
who with comfort to himself, indolently as it wer,   740
hath done as well; nay, for the very impediments
may ev'n be envied, as old navigators wer
in the glory they had got to hav outridden their storms.

IV

And yet from Zion's hill-top to the Dead-Sea shore,
between the Teacher sitting on the Mount and them,
the nethermost unfortunats, that cannot learn,—
in all the mid-mass crowding on the flowery slopes,
hearers o' the Word, ther is little difference to be told:
The same incarnat traitor routeth in all hearts;
nay, since 'tis an æsthetic delicacy of mind   750
that, refining the enticement of carnal pleasure,
voideth the shame, the elect are oft in straits extreme:
the mastery of warriorship, their apparent grace,
was won by disciplin of deadly strife: in them
ease is no indolence: indolence rather is theirs
who, ill-disposed to training, are unexercised
in good habit of war; and 'tis the lack thereof
maketh the soldier unready and the conflict so hard,
rather than any unwonted virulence or rage
of the onslaught; for thatt same happeneth anon to all.   760

AND here my thought plungeth into the darksome grove
and secret penetralia of ethic lore, wherein
I hav wander'd often and long and thought to know my way,
and now shall go retracing my remember'd paths,
tho' no lute ever sounded there nor Muse hath sung,

deviously in the obscure shadows, and none follow me
entering where erst I enter'd, and all enter free,
at the great clearing made by Socrates of yore,
when he said KNOW THYSELF; for true to his chief premiss
that ignorance is the root of all men's folly, he taught   770
to turn the lamp of Reason inwardly upon the mind.
And truly with thatt keen Γνῶθι σεαυτόν of his
was great felling of trees: for not Socrates knew
nor any hath ever kenn'd how man thinketh; and less
how thought thinketh itself; nor how in thatt province
Reason hath right to rule; nor of what stuff the reins
can be, wherewith the Charioteer bridled the steeds
in thatt same vision of his which Plato saith he told
to Phædrus, as they sat together on the banks
of the Ilissus talking of the passions of men.   780

All terrestrial Life, in all functions and motions,
operateth thru' alliance of living entities
disparat in their structure but logically
correlated in action under some final cause.
Suchlike co-ordinations may be acquired in man
with reason'd purpose consciently, as when a learner
on viol or flute diligently traineth his hand
to the intricat fingëring of the stops and strings;

or may be innate, as the spontaneous flight of birds;
or antenatal and altogether inconscient,   790
as the food-organs, call'd vegetativ because
such cellular connivance is the life of plants.

  The main co-ordinations whereon life hangeth
wer ever automatous, and such states when acquired·
tend to become self-working as they are perfected,
dropping out of our ken: the proverb truly spake
Habit is second nature, and 'twil function best
without superintendence, for the least brain-wave
or timid rippling of self-consciousness can rob

    the bodily movements of their nativ grace.   800
Now these perfected unify'd organities,
whether of inconscient birth or such as when acquired
proudly stand off from conscience, all act in response
to external stimulants that vary in kind, and range
from mere material contact to untraceable thought.

  Thus the digestiv kind is stirr'd by touch of food
within the body, or by the sight or sound or smell
of the object, or ev'n by the unconscious thought thereof;
and thence thru' appetite by mere thought of the sense;
and can decipher a message in the secret code   810
of language, and prick up at sound of the symbol:
For never can those privy-councilors in the brain

(165)

withhold official knowledge from the corporat mind;
ther is no deliberation or whisper'd thought, not ev'n
unspoken intention among them, but it wil leak out
to thatt swarming intelligence where life began,
and where ideas wander at liberty to find
their procreativ fellowship; thatt fluid sea
in which all problems, spiritual or logical ·
æsthetic mathematic or practic, resolve   820
melting as icebergs launch'd on the warm ocean-stream:
and wheresoe'er this corporat alchemy is at best,
'tis call'd by all men GENIUS, and its aptitudes
like virtuous disposition may be inherited.

  Thus must all kind of stimulus hav come some way
across the misty march-land, whereon men would fix
their disputable boundary between Matter and Mind,
—as every sensation must suffer translation
ere it can mediate in the live machinery
of any final cause or purpose: whence 'twould seem   830
that science went astray thinking to appropriate
some nervous reactions wholly to her material sphere,
and rather should hav thought to extend the mental field.

  Now this spontaneous life oweth nought to Reason
(the conscient faculty which Socrates invoked);
and so her claim to be the "very consciousness

of things judging themselves" is "vain above measure":
for every Essence hath its own Idea, and so
cometh thereby to its own full conscient life in man:
for-sure the idea of Beauty is not Reason's idea,　　　　840
nor hath Reason the idea of Courage or of Mirth,
of Faith or Love or Poetry or of Music's delight;
if Reason as an essence owneth to any idea,
let her make good her claim and therewith be content:
so be it; and surely Reason's property wil be
the idea of Order;—and if so, I think to find
how by the very natur of her own faculty
she was deceived to imagin its universal scope;
for since all natur is order'd (nor none wil deny
that 'tis by Reason alone we are of such order aware),　　　　850
all things must of their ordinance come in her court
for judgment; and 'twas thus Pythagoras coud hold
NUMBER to be the universal essence of things:
nay, see the starry atoms in the seed-plot of heav'n
stripp'd to their nakedness are nothing but Number;
and see how Mathematick rideth as a queen
cheer'd on her royal progress thru'out nature's realm;
see how physical Science, which is Reason's trade
and high profession, booketh ever and docketeth
all things in order and pattern; how Philosophy,　　　　860

shuttling out in the unknown like a hungry spider,
blindly spinneth her geometric webs, testing
and systematizing even her own disorders,
her solipsism and her gossamer ontologies
gnostic or cabbalist: and 'twas thus Socrates
coud evoke Reason to order and disciplin the mind—
the divine Logos that should shine in the darkness,—
a good physician who must heal himself withal.
[The assumed docility is by English moralists
term'd the 'Good Will' and fetch'd in as 'twer from without;
yet 'tis but the old animal instinct of selfhood   871
to'ard realization, which continueth on
with the animal promoted to spiritual life;
wherein desire for betterment is the promise
and premiss of all virtue; or if the willingness
be but desire of knowledge, thatt wil find the goal
where Truth and Virtue and Beauty are all as one.]
   Now seeing the aim of Socrates we must inquire
what the Mind's cóntents are; how disorder'd; and why
ther should in the good mind be any disorder at all.   880

What the Mind is, this thing bidden to know itself?
First I bethink me naturally of every man

as a unique creature, a personality
in whom we lucidly distinguish body and mind,
and talk readily of either tho' inseparable
and mutually dependent, together or apart
the created expression of Universal Mind.
And of the body I think as the machinery
of our terrestrial life evolving towards conscience
in the Ring of Reality; and thence of the mind   890
as thatt evolved conscience, the which in every-one
is different, as the body differeth also in each.

   And human Intellect I see form'd and compact
of the essential Ideas, wherewith soever each man
hath come in contact personally, and in so far
as he is kindly disposed to absorb their influences
to build his personality; and since all ideas
come to him thru' the senses, thatt old proviso
nisi ipse intellectus is futile to me;
for *intellectus* here seemeth to exclude itself,   900
as being thatt all-receptiv conscient energy
which is the mind of man; thatt ultimat issue
of the arch-creativ potency of Being, wherefrom
the senses took existence. Thus I come to think
that if the mind held all ideas in plenitude
'twould be complete, at one with natur and harmonized

with as good harmony as we may find in nature.

Now as our optic science teacheth pure white light
to be the consummation of all the color-bands
into which by diffraction it can be separated, 910
whereof if any ray went missing, the sunlight
wer impure and imperfect (or so we may think);
a suchlike imperfection must be in all men's minds,
because the complemental ideas parcel'd in each
are incomplete, being only such as thatt one man
may hav happ'd on, and those only in the measure whereby
he is tuned to take cognisance of them: thus it is
all men differ each from each, since neither environment
nor disposition can ever in any two men
be the same or alike, and therefor (as was said) 920
true individuality within the species
would seem reach'd in mankind. Again likewise 'tis seen
how national mentalities are mutually
incomprehensible and irreconcilable;
since each group as it rose was determin'd apart
by conditions of life which none other coud share,
by climate, language, and historic tradition
estranging evermore; nor are such obstinat bonds
the weaker for any intrinsic absurdity:
Nay, see the Armenian folk in their snow-burrows, 930

as if distrustful of their high mountainous plateau
between the seas, hav riveted their patriotism
by stubborn adherence to an ancient heresy,
a paradoxy anent the two natures of Christ,
which some theologic bishop, peering in the fog
of his own exhalations, thought pleasing to God;
altho' no creature might possibly understand it.

Again from this same cause it wil follow no less
that men commonly run so near to the average;
for the animal ideas are common property   940
and, being the greatest common measure of all mankind,
wil stand-out as the mean statistical features.

Again we now may see—and 'tis pleasant to see—
how simple characters hav such extreme beauty,
for that the soul's nobility consisteth not
in riches of imagination or intellect
but in harmony of Essences, which hath full power
where a few fundamentals in purity attain
their self-cöordination; as honest pots and pans
may for their unsophisticated beauty excell   950
a prize diploma-picture of our academy:
like as in music, when true voices blend in song,
the perfect intonation of the major triad
is sweetest of all sounds; its inviting embrace

resolveth all discords; and all the ambitious flights
of turbulent harmony come in the end to rest
with the fulfilment of its liquidating cloze.

Again we hence rebutt thatt old dilemma of Art,
which would set man in lordly enmity against nature
for that his pensiv play transcendeth her beauty;   960
—as when Sebastian preludeth, all her voices
that ever hav reach'd our ears are crest-fal'n and abash'd:
for tho' man cannot wield her infinit resource
of delicacy and strength, yet hath he in lieu thereof
a range triumphant, where his exorbitant thought
defying Space and Time hath power to blend all things
visible and invisible, and freely redispose
every essence that he knoweth, to parcel them at will—
or so he thinketh—, like an occult magician
whose summons all spirits must attend and obey,   970
from the heart-blaze of heaven to the unvisited deep;
tho' he hav no wizardry to exorcise them withal.
Now this dilemma (I say) is rebutted hereby,
because man's faculty of creation, rare in him
and not at his command, is but Nature herself,
who danceth in her garden at the blossöming-time
'mong the flowers of her setting; and tho' true it be
that Art needeth as full devotion and diligence

in the performance as doth Virtue, yet i' the mind
of the artist Nature's method surely is on this wise;—   980
the Ideas which thru' the senses hav found harborage,
being come to mortal conscience work-out of themselves
their right co-ordinations and, creativly
seeking expression, draw their natural imagery
from the same sensuous forms whereby they found entrance;
thus linking up with all the long tradition of Art.

    The manner of this magic is purest in musick,
but by the learner is seen more clearly in poetry,
wherein each verbal symbol exposeth its idea;
so that 'tis manifest by what promptings of thought   990
the imaginativ landscape is built and composed,
and how horizon'd: And the secret of a poem
lieth in this intimat echo of the poet's life.

    Now in its selfcreativness the manner of Art
cannot be simulated, altho' Mimicry
is Beauty's cradle: But, as in the Spirit of Man
all manner of grades are found, so wil it be in his Art,
with such disorder of thought as is not here to tell;
for every man, whom Beauty hath laid beneath her spell,
—tho' but by glimpse or dream, and him full ignorant   1000
of what idea hath moved him and ev'n by what means;—
wil feel about to express some mintage of himself,

by imitation or birdlike hymeneal lilt,
to fix his hold on joy, his COGITO ERGO SUM.
Thus may a jingle of words fasten his faith on God,
as schoolboys memorize their lesson better in rhyme.

Inasmuch then as the ideas in any one mind
are a promiscuous company muster'd at random,
ther wil be such disorder as Reason can perceive
and may hav skill to amend; but tho' we grant her art 1010
valid in principle and salutary in effect,
the debit of failure is heavy in her accounts.
Yet we discredit not all Medicine because
ther be incurable maladies that end in death,—
nor yet because the leech, when he is call'd in to heal
an indigestiv stomach, can hav no dealing
directly with the embroil'd co-ordinating cells,—
and, for the lack of any intelligent knowledge
of their intimat bickerings, wil hav recourse
to palliativs and sentimental assurances 1020
of favorable conditions, exercise and air,
hoping thus to entice them to a better behaviour,—
or observing some chemical excess in their chyme
wil deftly neutralize it with a pinch of salt;
so we shall also allow Reason her claim to rule:

and to judge by oneself, as each man must, I find
Reason wil diagnose the common ailment of Mind
a lack of harmony; for with the Ideas at war
—now one Idea in mastery and now another,
acting at call o' the moment indiscriminatly,—   1030
the man is foolish, unreasonable as we say,
inept, without set purpose, weak of will; whereas
if all should work together in concert, he wil be
determin'd and consistent: And I see man's Will
is here no independent concentrated force,
like the steel spring box'd-up in a French clock and wound
for local distribution, but is rather itself
the concentrating of a predistributed
intrinsic power;—the emotions, passions and desires,
concurrent with the Ideas, being surely of themselves   1040
wilful enough, and able among themselves at strife
to make a fool, and in co-ordination a sage.

    WILL, then, in the good mind a sustain'd harmony,
is in the bad a dissonance, or it may be a strange
co-ordination, or the tyranny of one idea;
from which our great civic convulsions mostly arise
and popular rebellions, when the Demagog
hath fulminated some mighty essential idea,
which entereth wildly into the loose minds of the herd

and, finding there no governance, runneth riot   1050

and, drawing all wilful authority to itself,

wil seem the only live thing; like a firebrand at night

flaring afar, that i' the sunlight wer a troublous smoke:

and if such insurrection by contagion attain

predominance uncontrollable, to the overthrow

of any existing rule, then the Will of the folk

is dubb'd by history's pen the WILL OF GOD.

But since this over-mastering prevalent idea

may be good in itself while it wreaketh but wrong,

and since I see that all human activities   1060

may be order'd equally for ravage or defence,

Reason herself here questioneth me how I trust

her mere ordering of life to make for happiness—

whereto my answer is my good faith in what I hav writ.

   How the mind of man from inconscient existence

cometh thru' the animal by growth of reasoning

to'ard spiritual conscience hath been duly told:

And Reason—being essentially (as in place 'twas found)

the idea of Order, and thus itself the appurtenance

of essences, with them passing from physical   1070

unto spiritual order in a mind endued

with conscience of the higher spiritual essences—

Reason (say I) wil rise to awareness of its rank

in the Ring of Existence, where man looketh up
to the first cause of all; and wil itself decree
and order discreetly the attitude of the soul
seeking self-realization in the vision of God,
becoming at the last thatt arch-conscience of all,
to which the Greek sage who possess'd it made appeal.

    The attraction of this motion is our conscience of it,   1080
our love of wisdom and of beauty; and the attitude
of those attracted wil be joyful obedience
with reverence to'ard the omnificent Creator
and First Cause, whose Being is thatt beauty and wisdom
which is to be apprehended only and only approach'd
by right understanding of his creation, and found
in thatt habit of faith which some thinkers hav styled
The Life of Reason; and this only true bond of love
and reasonable relation (if relation ther be)
'twixt creature and creator, man and nature's God,   1090
the which we call *Religion*,—is fundamental,
physically and metaphysically in fashion
or force undistinguishable from Duty itself:
sprung from the same primal reality, it also
aborted in like dolorous superstition, when
the first-born intimations of spiritual life
scared man's animal mind, that in childish terror

seeking protection from the unseen, fenced his dark cave
with codes of fearful fantasy and——flush'd by the stir
of the irresistible impulse which drave him (yea, still   1100
driveth) with fierce exultation (albeit we deplore
thatt barbarous aberration),——with credulous magic
cloggeth his airy spirit and discrediteth
his Reason and Faith alike . . . . . so old a trouble and great
that the honest indictment of the Epicurean
goeth unrefuted, and his famous verse TANTUM
RELIGIO POTUIT SUADERE MALORUM
yet ringeth true as when he thought to benefit
mankind, and from his woes rescue him for ever,
drowning the thought of God from off the face of the earth   1110
in his deluge of atoms; and made in the mind
a second Void, the which his sect should keep inane
by the inventiv levity of their enlightenment;
til, as with animals that hav fasted too long
and aking within for their emptiness wil eat
too greedily, we see in our fellows today
fresh recrudescence of forgonn superstition;
the while our generation, sicken'd by the grime
of murky slums, slag-heaps and sooty bushes,
wil plan garden-cities and for her soilure make .   1120
reddition to Nature, replanting the fair lands

which our industrial grandsires disaforested.

    This hankering after lost Beauty, in sickness of heart
a disconsolat sentiment, is the remnant grace
of nature's covenant, the starved germ *athirst for God
ev'n for the living God*, that singeth in the psalm
QUEMADMODUM CERVUS, and now amidst the blank
tyranny of ugliness maketh many a rebel
pining for enlargement and plotting to recall
thatt old arrant exile who, for all her mischief,   1130
hid neath her cloak the master-key of happiness.

    In truth "spiritual animal" wer a term for man
nearer than "rational" to define his genus;
Faith being the humanizer of his brutal passions,
the clarifier of folly and medicine of care,
the clue of reality, and the driving motiv
of thatt self-knowledge which teacheth the ethick of life.

    And yet hath PRAYER, the heav'n-breathing foliage of faith,
found never a place in ethick: for Philosophy
filtering out delusions from her theory of life,   1140
in dread of superstition gave religion away
to priests and monks, who rich in their monopoly
furbish and trim the old idols, that they darè not break,
for fear of the folk and need of good disciplin.

But since all men alike, in any strain of heart
or great emotion of soul, credulous or sceptic, fall
instinctivly to prayer for thatt solace and strength
which they who use the habit may be seen to hav found—
nay, had Prayer no effect other than reverence
for the self-knowledge, which the Greek enjoin'd, whereby
'tis sovran to bind character, concentrate Will,   1151
and purify intention—nay, ev'n so 'twould claim
a place among the causes of determin'd flux.

  Ah! tho' it may be a simple thing in reach of all,
Best ever is rare, a toilsome guerdon; and prayer is like
those bodily exercises that athletes wil use,
which each must humbly learn, and ere he win to power
so diligently practise, and in such strict course
as wil encroach unkindly on the agreements of life:
whence men slouch in the laxity that they call ease,   1160
rather than rouse to acquiring thatt strength, without which
the body cannot know the pleasur of its full ease,
  the leisur of strength in the hard labor of life.

Now every emotion hath the bodily expression
beseeming each; and since the body cannot be
without some attitude, so Prayer wil hav its own:
and here just as in any athletic exercise

ther be postures and motions foolish in themselves
and often undignified, so too the postur of prayer
may shame our pride of spirit, which would grudge the limbs
warrant of entry upon her sacred solitudes;   1171
albeit the body come there in full abject guize
to do submission and pay fealty to the soul:
And since our speech, in its mere vocal cries and calls,
hath less natural beauty and true significance
than the bodily gestures which convey our desires,
so ev'n the words of prayer wil lack in dignity
and seem impertinent; as full often they be,
and ever had been, unless man's language had upgrown
from makeshift unto mastery of his thought, and learn'd   1180
by its fine musing art to redeem for his soul
the beauty of holiness, marrying creativly
his best earthly delight with his heav'nliest desire,
when he calleth on God, *Send forth thy light and truth*
that they may lead me and bring me unto thy Holy Hill,
to thatt fair place which is *the joy of the whole earth.*
  See! ther is never dignity in a concourse of men,
save only as some spiritual gleam hearteneth the herd.
Any idea whatsoe'er new-born to consciousness,
if it infect the folk, taketh repetend life   1190
and exuberant difformity of disorder'd growth

from physical communion of emotion and thought;
and of its nàscent appetency 'twil embrace
affinity in its host, to stagger and eliminate
all other ideas, thus improportionably
surmounting its own province in Nature's order;
so that unless itself it be a thing of Beauty,
insurmountable of kind, more beauteous in excess—
as when the glow reverberating in a golden cup
multiplyeth the splendour,—it cometh that the herd,   1200
being in its empassionment ever irrational,
wil even of harmless enthusiasm breed disgrace.

   Thus in our English sport, the spectacular games,
where tens of thousands flock throttling the entrance-gates
like sheep to th' pen, wherein they sit huddled to watch
the fortune o' the football, ther is often here and there
mid the seething glomeration of thatt ugly embankment
of gazing faces, one that came to enjoy the sight
knowingly, and yet looketh little on the contest: to him
the crowd is the spectacle; its wrestle and agony   1210
is more than the actors, and its contagion so thick
and irresistible, that ere he feel surprise
he too may find himself, yea philosophy and all,
carried away—as when a strong swimmer in the sea
who would regain the shore, is by the headlong surf

toss'd out of action, and like a drifted log roll'd up
breathless and unresisting on the roaring beach.

But if he join the folk, when at the cloze of Lent
they kneel in the vast dimness of a city church,
while on the dense silence the lector's chant treadeth   1220
from cadence to cadence the long dolorous way
of the great passion of Christ,—or anon when they rise
to free their mortal craving in the exultant hymn
that ringeth with far promise of eternal peace . . .
or should it happen to him, in strange lands far from home,
to watch the Moslem host, when at their hour of prayer
they troop in wild accoutrement their long-drill'd line
motionless neath the sun upon the Arabian sands,
hush'd to th' Imám's solemnel invocation of God,
as their proud tribal faith savagely draweth strength   1230
from the well-spring of life,—then at the full Amen
of their deep-throated respond he wil feel his spirit
drawn into kinship and their exaltation his own;
the more that he himself can be no part thereof,
incomprehensible because comprehending:
—and they be muddied pools whereat the herd water.

Such is the dignity of prayer in the common folk;
and its humility is the robe of intellect.
So whenever it hath been by some mystics renounced

in sanctuary of their sublime abstraction—as if   1240

utter abnegation had left no manners else to abjure,—

they appear to lack in use and duty of fellowship.

Yet in such solitaries, pallid clerks of heaven,

souls blanch'd for lack of sunjoys (as 'twould seem to hav been),

their contemplation (it may be) of very intensity

generateth ideas of higher irradiance;

for ideas born to human personality,

having their proper attractions like as atom or cell,

from soul to soul pass freely; and 'twas this mystery,

whereof they kenn'd the need who set that clause i' the creed,

which, compelling belief in the COMMUNION OF SAINTS,   1251

foldeth the sheep in pastures of eternal life.

Nor doubt I that as this thinking machinery

perisheth with the body, so animal thought

with all its whimper and giggle must perish therewith,

with all shames, all vain ostentation and ugliness,

and all personality of all other ideas;

except it be that, like as in unconscient things

whence conscience came, ther is also thru' out conscient life

the same emergent evolution, persisting   1260

in our spiritual life to the goal of conscience.

   This mind perisheth with this body, unless

the personal co-ordination of its ideas
hav won to Being higher than animal life,
at thatt point where the Ring cometh upward to reach
the original creativ Energy which is God,
with conscience entering into life everlasting.

'TWAS at thatt hour of beauty when the setting sun
squandereth his cloudy bed with rosy hues, to flood
his lov'd works as in turn he biddeth them Good-night;   127c
and all the towers and temples and mansions of men
face him in bright farewell, ere they creep from their pomp
naked beneath the darkness;—while to mortal eyes
'tis given, ifso they close not of fatigue, nor strain
at lamplit tasks—'tis given, as for a royal boon
to beggarly outcasts in homeless vigil, to watch
where uncurtain'd behind the great windows of space
Heav'n's jewel'd company circleth unapproachably—
    'Twas at sunset that I, fleeing to hide my soul
in refuge of beauty from a mortal distress,   1280
walk'd alone with the Muse in her garden of thought,
discoursing at liberty with the mazy dreams
that came wavering pertinaciously about me; as when
the small bats, issued from their hangings, flitter o'erhead

thru' the summer twilight, with thin cries to and fro
hunting in muffled flight atween the stars and flowers.

  Then fell I in strange delusion, illusion strange to tell;
for as a man who lyeth fast asleep in his bed
may dream he waketh, and that he walketh upright
pursuing some endeavour in full conscience—so 'twas   1290
with me;'but contrawise; for being in truth awake
methought I slept and dreamt; and in thatt dream methought
I was telling a dream; nor telling was I as one
who, truly awaked from a true sleep, thinketh to tell
his dream to a friend, but for his scant remembrances
findeth no token of speech—it was not so with me;
for my tale was my dream and my dream the telling,
and I remember wondring the while I told it
how I told it so tellingly. And yet now 'twould seem
that Reason inveigled me with her old orderings;   1300
as once when she took thought to adjust theology,
peopling the inane that vex'd her between God and man
with a hierarchy of angels; like those asteroids
wherewith she later fill'd the gap 'twixt Jove and Mars.

  Verily by Beauty it is that we come at WISDOM,
yet not by Reason at Beauty: and now with many words
pleasing myself betimes I am fearing lest in the end
I play the tedious orator who maundereth on

for lack of heart to make an end of his nothings.
Wherefor as when a runner who hath run his round   1310
handeth his staff away, and is glad of his rest,
here break I off, knowing the goal was not for me
the while I ran on telling of what cannot be told.

For not the Muse herself can tell of Goddes love;
which cometh to the child from the Mother's embrace,
an Idea spacious as the starry firmament's
inescapable infinity of radiant gaze,
that fadeth only as it outpasseth mortal sight:
and this direct contact is 't with eternities,
this springtide miracle of the soul's nativity   1320
that oft hath set philosophers adrift in dream;
which thing Christ taught, when he set up a little child
to teach his first Apostles and to accuse their pride,
saying, *Unless ye shall receive it as a child,*
ye cannot enter into the kingdom of heaven.
So thru'out all his young mental apprenticehood
the child of very simplicity, and in the grace
and beauteous attitude of infantine wonder,
is apt to absorb Ideas in primal purity,
and by the assimilation of thatt immortal food   1330
may build immortal life; but ever with the growth

(187)

of understanding, as the sensible images

are more and more corrupt, troubled by questioning thought,

or with vainglory alloy'd, 'tis like enough the boy

in prospect of his manhood wil hav cast to th' winds

his Baptism with his Babyhood; nor might he escape

the fall of Ev'ryman, did not a second call

of nature's Love await him to confirm his Faith

or to revoke him if he is wholly lapsed therefrom.

    And so mighty is this second vision, which cometh   1340

in puberty of body and adolescence of mind

that, forgetting his Mother, he calleth it "first Love";

for it mocketh at suasion or stubbornness of heart,

as the oceantide of the omnipotent Pleasur of God,

flushing all avenues of life, and unawares

by thousandfold approach forestalling its full flood

with divination of the secret contacts of Love,—

of faintest ecstacies aslumber in Nature's calm,

like thought in a closed book, where some poet long since

sang his throbbing passion to immortal sleep—with coy   1350

tendernesses delicat as the shifting hues

that sanctify the silent dawn with wonder-gleams,

whose evanescence is the seal of their glory,

consumed in self-becoming of eternity;

til every moment as it flyeth, cryeth "Seize!

Seize me ere I die! I am the Life of Life."

'Tis thus by near approach to an eternal presence
man's heart with divine furor kindled and possess'd
falleth in blind surrender; and finding therewithal
in fullest devotion the full reconcilement   1360
betwixt his animal and spiritual desires,
such welcome hour of bliss standeth for certain pledge
of happiness perdurable: and coud he sustain
this great enthusiasm, then the unbounded promise
would keep fulfilment; since the marriage of true minds
is thatt once fabled garden, amidst of which was set
the single Tree that bore such med'cinable fruit
that if man ate thereof he should liv for ever.

Friendship is in loving rather than in being lov'd,
which is its mutual benediction and recompense;   1370
and tho' this be, and tho' love is from lovers learn'd,
it springeth none the less from the old essence of self.
No friendless man ('twas well said) can be truly himself;
what a man looketh for in his friend and findeth,
and loving self best, loveth better than himself,
is his own better self, his live lovable idea,
flowering by expansion in the loves of his life.

And in the nobility of our earthly friendships
we hav all grades of attainment, and the best may claim

perfection of kind; and so, since ther be many bonds   1380
other than breed (friendships of lesser motiv, found
even in the brutes) and since our politick is based
on actual association of living men, 'twil come
that the spiritual idea of Friendship, the huge
vastidity of its essence, is fritter'd away
in observation of the usual habits of men;
as happ'd with the great moralist, where his book saith
that ther can be no friendship betwixt God and man
because of their unlimited disparity.

From this dilemma of pagan thought, this poison of faith,
Man-soul made glad escape in the worship of Christ;   1391
for his humanity is God's Personality,
and communion with him is the life of the soul.

Of which living ideas (when in the struggle of thought
harden'd by language they became symbols of faith)
Reason builded her maze, wherefrom none should escape,
wandering intent to map and learn her tortuous clews,
chanting their clerkly creed to the high-echoing stones
of their-hand fashion'd temple: but the Wind of heav'n
bloweth where it listeth, and Christ yet walketh the earth,
and talketh still as with those two disciples once   1401
on the road to Emmaus—where they walk and are sad;
whose vision of him then was his victory over death,

thatt resurrection which all his lovers should share,
who in loving him had learn'd the Ethick of happiness;
whereby they too should come where he was ascended
to reign over men's hearts in the Kingdom of God.

Our happiest earthly comradeships hold a foretaste
of the feast of salvation and by thatt virtue in them
provoke desire beyond them to out-reach and surmount   1410
their humanity in some superhumanity
and ultimat perfection: which, howe'er 'tis found
or strangely imagin'd, answereth to the need of each
and pulleth him instinctivly as to a final cause.
Thus unto all who hav found their high ideal in Christ,
Christ is to them the essence discern'd or undiscern'd
of all their human friendships; and each lover of him
and of his beauty must be as a bud on the Vine
and hav participation in him; for Goddes love
is unescapable as nature's environment,   1420
which if a man ignore or think to thrust it off
he is the ill-natured fool that runneth blindly on death.

This Individualism is man's true Socialism.
This is the rife Idea whose spiritual beauty
multiplieth in communion to transcendant might.
This is thatt excelent way whereon if we wil walk
all things shall be added unto us—thatt Love which inspired

the wayward Visionary in his dóctrinal ode
to the three christian Graces, the Church's first hymn
and only deathless athanasian creed,—the which   1430
    "except a man believe he cannot be savèd".
This is the endearing bond whereby Christ's company
yet holdeth together on the truth of his promise
that he spake of his great pity and trust in man's love,
Lo, I am with you always ev'n to the end of the world.
    Truly the Soul returneth the body's loving
where it hath won it . . . and God so loveth the world . . .
and in the fellowship of the friendship of Christ
God is seen as the very self-essence of love,
Creator and mover of all as activ Lover of all,   1440
self-express'd in not-self, without which no self were.
In thought whereof is neither beginning nor end
nor space nor time; nor any fault nor gap therein
'twixt self and not-self, mind and body, mother and child,
'twixt lover and loved, God and man: but ONE ETERNAL
in the love of Beauty and in the selfhood of Love.

Lightning Source UK Ltd.
Milton Keynes UK
26 August 2010

159033UK00001B/151/A